Advance Praise for The '

This is a book of wisdom garnered over decades of work with gifted children. It is also a call for radical change in our understanding of education and a passionate plea to discover and honor both the essence of the individual child and the interconnectedness of us all. A must read from one of our most gifted elders!
    —Stephanie S. Tolan, M.A.
        Newbery Honor winning author and co-author of *Guiding the Gifted Child*

For over sixty years, Annemarie Roeper has envisioned a world that honors the growth of the Self. In this book, she combines the wisdom of experience with the stories of children and invites us to explore a judgment free process that encourages the discovery and evolution of the true Self in an environment of openness and love.
    —Michele Kane, Ed.D.
        Coordinator of Gifted Programs Antioch CCSD #34,
        and Core Group Member, Qualitative Assessment

A visionary book capturing the real changes in consciousness that have been noted in gifted children throughout the world. Annemarie invites us to explore with her the inner depths of human experience—the mystical and mysterious Self. She gives us a template for entering a child's world without judgment, discovering the inner agenda of this precious Self, and nourishing its development.
    —Linda Kreger Silverman, Ph.D.
        Director, Gifted Development Center
        Denver, Colorado

This is the most beautiful book about gifted children. Each sentence speaks volumes of truth about their emotions that we don't even suspect are there. From the inspired allegory of the Self in Dialogue to the concept of Legitimacy, this little book calls to us to be read and reread so that we may absorb its profound perspective on children's emotional and spiritual reality. This book is also unique in that almost all the examples are of young children. Annemarie Roeper then does a remarkable fast forward to Growing Up Gifted, a new topic to us all.
    —Michael M. Piechowski, Ph.D.
        author of *Mellow Out, They Say. If I Only Could. Intensities and Sensitivities of the Young and Bright*

The "I" of the Beholder:
A Guided Journey to the Essence of a Child

Annemarie Roeper
with Ann Higgins

Great Potential Press, Inc.
Scottsdale, Arizona

The "I" of the Beholder: A Guided Journey to the Essence of a Child

Cover design: Linda Longmire Design
Interior design: The Printed Page
Copy editing: Jennifer Ault

Published by Great Potential Press, Inc.
P.O. Box 5057
Scottsdale, AZ 85261

Printed on recycled paper

11 10 09 08 07   5 4 3 2 1

Library of Congress Cataloging-in-Publication Data

Roeper, Annemarie, 1918-
   The "I" of the beholder : a guided journey to the essence of a child
/ Annemarie Roeper.
      p. cm.
   Includes bibliographical references.
   ISBN 0-910707-78-2
  1. Gifted children. 2. Gifted children--Education. 3. Child psychology.
4. Self in children. 5. Self-actualization (Psychology) in children. I.
Title.
   HQ773.5.R64 2007
   155.4--dc22

                           2006032700

ISBN 13: 978-0-910707-78-7
ISBN 10: 0-910707-78-2

I dedicate this book to my great-grandson,
due in November 2006

Giftedness is a greater awareness, a greater sensitivity,
and a greater ability to understand and transform perceptions
into intellectual and emotional experiences.

Annemarie Roeper

Acknowledgments

This book would not have come into being without the wonderful and continued assistance of Ann Higgins. It was because of her that I was able to get my spoken thoughts down on paper. Her insights and gentle questioning helped me refine my ideas, and some of the words in this book are hers. She is a longtime companion who has become a trusted friend, and I appreciate her immensely.

This book has gone through many incarnations, and with each, different people participated and helped. It began at the home of Hilton and Linda Silverman probably 10 years ago with Linda's encouragement. An early version was put together with much help and thought from Ellen Fiedler. Michelle Kane and Betty Meckstroth made helpful contributions. All through its growth and development, there was Michael Piechowski: thoughtful, critical, and supportive. I would also like to thank Debbie Russell, my assistant, and Lois Peterson. My heartfelt thanks to them all, as well as to my children and grandchildren, who are always ready to support me in my changing moods.

Foreword

Annemarie Roeper has a beautiful worldview that finds its expression in her prescriptions for parenting and educating children. But her philosophy applies to many other arenas of life, such as politics, economics, ethics. She is the champion of global awareness, interdependence, and self-actualization. Her philosophy is profound, yet concrete enough that it serves as a foundation for several schools. Her impact on education could equal Maria Montessori's. Annemarie's blueprint of the psyche will also guide parents in developing the unique Selves of their children. If world leaders were to heed the ideas in this book, the Self of every human being on the planet would be honored, and we should inhabit an ideal world.

Linda K. Silverman, Ph.D.
Director, Gifted Development Center
Denver, Colorado

Contents

Preface

I was born in Vienna, Austria, on August 27, 1918. I was told that I spent the first three months of my life being carried back and forth to the hospital where my mother was a medical student working toward becoming a psychoanalyst.

I grew up during a time of great cultural excitement, which was particularly evident in the cities of Prague and Vienna. Many outstanding authors, musicians, artists, and medical doctors worked during this period. One of the most outstanding was Sigmund Freud, whose theories I drank in with my mother's milk, for she would nurse me while discussing theory with her psychoanalyst friends. There was an atmosphere of great excitement about and emphasis on ideas about the psyche.

There was also a great emphasis on thoughtful education for children. It was a period when boarding schools sprang up all over Europe, each one filled with new approaches; Summerhill was one of the most well-known, but it was only one of many exciting new experiments in education. Marienau, the boarding school my parents created, was very much in the new wave of thinking about education.[1] It united two streams of thought: psychoanalysis and education—each a specialty of one of my parents. Their gifts extended into the arts as well. Both of my parents were excellent pianists, and my father received his Ph.D. in art history. With these extraordinary backgrounds, my parents hoped to create a totally new generation of children based on highly developed community living. They created Marienau on a large farm property for a "back-to-nature" take on a pantheistic belief in the sanctity of life.

It was in this truly idealistic environment where I had my first life experiences. I made friends; I learned to read and sing and dance; I learned to respect and love nature. I finished what would be the equivalent of American high school there and went on to medical studies at the University of Vienna.

It all ended abruptly, however, in the year 1933, when Hitler took over Germany. My family lost everything it had built up over 30 years and, more seriously, everything it had so hopefully believed in. For me, it was such a great shock that to this day I have yet to truly overcome it. I was in the midst of my studies in medicine at the University, on my way to becoming a psychoanalyst, when Hitler came to power and I had to abandon it all, fleeing my country and my idyllic life, leaving much behind.

The saving grace was that we were able to transplant all of our ideas to America, where we created several schools. None of it would have been possible without the courage and insight of my husband, George Roeper, for he was the one who foresaw the tragedy and made our transition to the United States possible. Together we created Roeper School, which still promotes the same philosophy of community and support of the Self of the child. Even though I never went back to university studies, George and I each received honorary Ed.D. degrees from Eastern Michigan University in 1978. Our three children, and now three grandchildren, were all born in the United States. A great-grandchild will be born soon, so my family continues.

It was around the 1950s that George and I became aware of the specific needs of gifted children, and we slowly changed Roeper School into a school for the gifted. George and I retired from the Roeper School around 1980 after running it for 35 years, and he passed away in 1992. After my husband's death, I continued to work in the same direction and developed an alternative approach to assessing gifted children called "Qualitative Assessment," based on the recognition that gifted children are not only cognitively different, but also emotionally and spiritually different as well.

Roeper School continues to thrive and be a haven for children who are gifted. The school still holds the philosophy that each child has a unique Self that should be honored. I hope the school will continue for many more years.

I now live in El Cerrito, California, and have found other ways to continue the work of my parents and my husband. The pain of losing George was mitigated somewhat by the fact that I had found a wonderful circle of friends, most of whom are part of the core group who helped create the structure of the Qualitative Assessment approach. I am glad to write this book, which explains more about my personal philosophy, educational approaches, and the Qualitative Assessment method. I hope it will prompt parents and educators to rethink many practices that are common today but which can actually be harmful for gifted children.

Annemarie M. Roeper
September 2006

Introduction

What drives me to write this book? Perhaps it is a sense of the mystery of life, the mystery of the universe that surrounds us, and the mystery that is within us. It is within these vast unknowns that we try to establish our identities. We strive to carve out a place that is known, a place that we can manage, a place that is safe, a place that allows us to grow our unique Selves. This is nothing less than our struggle for psychic survival, a need for identity: tribal identity, national identity, group identity, a family identity, and finally, an individual identity.

Perhaps I am writing this book because I have seen how humanity is hurting its children. We have failed to create a safe, harmonious society for past, current, and future generations. History is made in the cradle and in the classroom, and how a child grows, how his or her Self develops, determines the future of our world. We lack a fundamental understanding of the human soul and how it develops. This lack of understanding affects every aspect of our lives, whether it is politics, economics, education, the penal system, or relations between the nations of the world. In our approach to children and ourselves, we need a view that includes the Self and the universal reality of physical and spiritual interdependence. This book offers a new model to guide us in honoring our complex, mysterious Self.

The Self is a complex unit, filled with conscious and unconscious reactions, drives, feelings, and anxieties. These component parts of the Self have their origin in our DNA, our history, and our experiences, as well as the deeper, more mysterious aspects of existence. The inner agenda of our unique Self is what drives us. It is the final power in the world. It will not be swayed by society's concept of reason. We need a blueprint of the psyche that honors the Self in all its aspects and that understands our universal interdependence.

A strange thing happened to this book as it developed a life of its own and came closer to experiencing its own birth. Its real purpose emerged. It expresses and conveys the enormous, passionate, unbearable longing of the world's people to experience this Earth as their true home, the place where they belong in safety and openness, where there is harmony and integrity between life on earth and the mysteries of this world. Personally, I have felt this longing all my life as an ache, a desire that could never be stilled. While I could overrule or suppress it at times, it was always present. When I set out to write this book, I knew I was taking on the task of giving voice to this longing. I also knew that to succeed, I would need an expanded horizon.

I needed to find ways to be able to say "yes" to the mystery of this world. Science, with its need to prove, was not the answer. Religion, too, often failed to solve the contradiction between its lofty goals and human frailty. I felt as if I would have to set out on this journey of hope and longing alone. Even as I hoped for a worldview that would be accepted by others, I worried that few seemed to share my goals, and I despaired that my dream might never be fulfilled.

Yet slowly, an unexpected light appeared on the horizon. Unnoticed by most, the first signs of change came with the millennium. I began to notice mysterious changes, at least in the environments that I am most familiar with. Many others, too, began to notice the increasingly frequent appearance of a new type of child. More and more highly gifted children came to our attention. Each amazed us with distinct cognitive and emotional characteristics and an apparent philosophy of life. As my book filled up with examples and experiences, I realized that children and their parents were changing both in their character and their attitudes.

Simultaneously, the horrible war in Iraq broke out, and a huge global peace movement was born. Both the peace movement and the new children based their thoughts and feelings on a different, expanded worldview. All of a sudden, things were happening which this book had been trying to work toward without much hope of ever actually achieving. These phenomena—ranging from a global peace movement to gifted children—embodied what I had been so fervently trying to express as I wrote this book.

Personally, this sudden recognition led to the most contradictory emotions: despair over the terrible tragedies of war and our loss of personal liberties in this country, and deep joy over the expanded horizon. As my worldview expanded, the perspective of the book changed. I understood that these changes would bring unexpected challenges and wondered how I would meet these challenges.

One challenge has been to describe emotions in such a way that other people can feel them. I would like the reader to keep in mind that words can only approximate the complexity of the Self.

A major purpose of this book is to put the spotlight on the dichotomy between the goals of society and the goals of the Self, and the enormous impact of the conflict between the two. Society fails to recognize the importance of the Self, and as a result, society as a whole is typically puzzled by the mysteries of individual human behavior. Society tries to mold the Self toward its purposes. The human Self, on the other hand, is driven toward the protection of its integrity and unity, as well as its growth and development. Each living being has the power of an inner passion to make an impact on the world. Each human being also has his or her own "I," which is the beholder, and fashions a passionate reaction according to his or her own vision. Our Selves are not governed by reason alone, but also by our passion and power. In this book, I will examine this vision, this passion, and this power—the indomitable spirit of the individual "I" that is able to resist all so-called rhyme and reason in order to protect itself. Every detail of our lives is governed by this struggle for survival of the Self within the context of the universe. If we fail to understand the "I," our limited point of view will cause us to inflict injury on each other's Selves.

In this book, I will describe the complexity of the Self as the source of all human behavior. I will try to outline the structure of the Self, its normal growth and development, and the role of interaction with other living things in this process. I see the Self as a unit within us, which includes input from the brain and all other functions of the body. This book will explore how the inclusion of the concept of "soul" or "psyche" or "Self"[2] can change the methods, priorities, and goals of society and parenting. This, in turn, could change how we view each child and ourselves and have an impact on our every action and reaction, whether in the boardroom, the bedroom, or the classroom.[3]

Chapter 1

The Self, Its Existence, and Its Power

Whether life will continue on this world now depends on us.
And whether we survive, and preserve a life worth living,
depends on the kind of selves we are able to create, and on
the social forms that we succeed in building.

~ Mihaly Csikszentmihalyi[4]

These thoughts about the Self of the human being have been ripening in me for many, many years. Their pressure to be born was almost unbearable. I needed to share my vision, my experiences, my perception of this wonderful and terrible world. I needed to explore the strange phenomenon of the Self and how strongly it impacts our lives and the lives of those around us.

Yet this book almost died before it could see the light of day. Why? The answer finally came to me. Because I had been trying to define the Self in cognitive terms, the essence of what I set out to describe eluded me again and again. Something was always missing in my descriptions. It was as though something kept knocking at my door, saying, "Don't leave me out; I am essential."

I finally opened the door, and there was the human Self. It said, "May I introduce myself? I am the "I" of the beholder, the inside that looks out at the outside. I am the missing link to your understanding of the human being. I am the passion, the power, the creative force that looks out of the eyes of children, and I have been standing out in the cold for a long time. My stomach is empty. My growth has been stunted; my voice, ignored. You must stop speaking *about* me and speak *with* me and include me in your plans and your thinking.

"Stop judging me, evaluating me, categorizing me. I am an enigma and will remain one. If you include me, we can dance together. If not, I will shrink and be crippled and cower in the corner. The strength of my feelings will be undiminished, but if they have no outlet, they might burst out in destructive ways.

"I am wondering how words could describe my complexity and mystery. How can cognitive terms explain what you see in the trusting, eager eyes of children who look at you expecting safety and comfort, unconditional love, and true empathy? In their eyes, you can see such depth of feeling, such thirst for growth, such creativity, and a passion for learning.

"Each one is filled with unpredictable mystery, drive, and potential—a complete agenda of his own. And such beauty! But also uncertainty, questions, fear, anger, jealousy, distrust. Their eyes and ways truly speak volumes, if you know how to read them. It is the Self, the 'I' of the beholder that looks at you from these eyes. I, the Self, say to you, I trust you to help me develop and become who I am, who I want to be, who I am destined to be.

"I don't want to be crippled. I don't want to turn my excitement for living into aggression or sadness. I need support so that I can take my tentative steps until I learn to walk unaided. I need help so I can grow. I need to spread my wings so I can fly.

"I, the young Self, unabashedly bring my feelings to you. Does not that awaken your own feelings? Are you touched by my beauty and trust, power and passion, uniqueness and complexity? This tender growth can easily be sidetracked from its triumphant progress by other Selves, blind institutions, and adults who have attention deficit when it comes to attending to the Self. I hope that your readers identify with my feelings. It is against this background of feelings that you must express your thoughts about me, the Self."

I asked, "How can I do this? What will I tell my readers? They want me to give them a prescription about how to help you grow and spread your wings."

As I spoke, the Self grew and filled the room, and it spread beyond the room. It said to me, "I am a whole world, the inside which confronts the outside and wants to be one with it. But I am trapped inside and can only reach out to you if the world outside understands me and feels with me.

"Find a way to make people understand me and all the other Selves, especially children's Selves, which are so tiny and vulnerable. Humankind needs to learn about me, my power, and my complexity. Make me visible, for I need to grow just as the physical body does. Just like the physical body, I, too, need food and shelter. I need to be cared for. Let them know that they must respect me, for the fate of the world depends on the Selves of human beings."

"How can I define that which is indefinable?" I asked. Then I had a thought. "Do you mean make a model of you?"

"Yes, translate me into a way people can recognize me. Tell them that there is much to learn about me and that the knowledge can be helpful to understand me from the inside out. You are driven to describe me. I have been stirring up your emotions for years now. Promise me you will find a way to do this."

I promised, and here is the result.

I said, "Let's do it together, like we do everything together, for one of the strange things that we humans can do is to look at our own Selves from the outside in, as well as from the inside out. In other words, we can feel and at the same time watch our Selves feeling."

The Self was astonished, and our dialogue continued.

"Let's pretend," I said, "that you are one of the organs of the body, that you are a separate entity, yet vitally connected with all the other body parts."

The Self warmed up to this approach and got very excited. "What is the task of the organs inside the body?"

I answered, "They each have a different task. The job of each is clearly defined. They each contribute their part to the whole of the body. To fulfill this task, they need to protect themselves from harm. So one of the tasks is self-protection. Another task is to maintain the connection to the whole body."

"What is my task? How does it differ from those organs?" asked the Self.

"You are the core of our being; all of the other parts of the body are felt to be part of you. When any part of the body is hurt, you feel hurt. When our body feels well, you feel well. We know we are alive because we feel ourselves as 'I.' I have never died, but I know it is the 'I' that feels the dying. It is the 'I' that stops existing in the form in which we are used to when we die."

"And the 'I' is me," said the Self, astounded, "and I know myself. Yet I do not know much about myself. I am so important, and yet I am invisible."

"That is right," I said, "and the two of us—who are really one—are becoming more and more comfortable with each other. We are getting to know each other."

"And now we are back to the question of how to make me visible."

"I think I know the answer," I said. "A child gave me the clue. If you knew her, you would know that you are not really invisible. She actually saw you."

"How did she see me if I am invisible?" asked the Self.

"It is really simple. All you need is a little imagination." The Self looked dubious. I said, "I will tell you a true story. A few years ago, I worked with an eight-year-old who had difficulties in school. She showed me a picture she had drawn and said, 'This picture will tell you why I am having trouble.' I saw a small child in a car but could not tell what she was talking about by looking at the picture. She said, 'You will need this,' and handed me a magnifying glass. Now I could tell. There was a picture of the Earth inside the child's head, with hot flames shooting out of it. She said, 'There's a whole world inside of me that doesn't match with the world outside, and that is why I am having trouble.' She said this is what makes her so lonely and helpless and angry. She said the world inside every person is as big as the one outside, only no one knows that it is there."

"All that is me?" asked the Self, when it saw the picture of the world in the child's head. "I did not know there was so much of me. Only I think I live in the heart and not in the head. At least that is where I feel myself to be."

"Why don't we assume that you are in the heart? It feels right to me."

Again the Self spoke up, "How can we show this to the world?"

"You just saw what imagination can do, and imagination is another reality. It is like magic. Let us pretend that we are taking an x-ray picture of you as we do the body's organs."

All of a sudden, we saw a huge screen in front of our inner eyes. On it was a breathtaking picture in sound and color and movement. There were different layers, constantly changing— mountains and valleys and oceans, sunshine and darkness, hidden crevices, round-nesses, openings and closings. Some beautiful, quiet landscapes shone brightly; others were stormy, wind-blown, trembling with earth-quakes, and zigzagged with lightning. There were holes spewing fire. The strangest thing was that most of it was in darkness, some in semi-darkness. Then we could see the surface breaking, streaks of light going in and out, and a whole layer totally visible and in constant motion.

The Self watched in awe as the picture unfolded. The Self in the picture seemed to have certain shape and form, but one end of it seemed to be endless and disappeared into infinity. That part was dark.

"All of that is me?" asked the Self. It seemed proud for the first time. "So I really do exist? I was not quite sure, for sometimes I feel nobody notices me." The Self watched itself in awe. But then it said, "What is all this inside of me? What is this motion? All this activity? It looks as though there is as much going on inside of me as outside. I seem to have an exciting inner life."

"Did you see all of those objects flying right out of the picture?" I asked. "Those are the connections with the outside. Some combine well with the outside; others get locked in violent struggle."

"Yes," said the Self, "I have experienced that many times. It felt as though I was being squashed, or lifted up and allowed to shine. But I still don't understand what I am seeing. Is it like a movie? Is there a plot?"

"In a way, you could say that," I answered. "You have your own agenda, your inner mandate. This mandate originates from all sorts of sources. It moves in all sorts of directions but functions as a unit. It becomes a life force. You are destined to grow a certain way, as is the flower and all living beings. Sometimes flowers persist in growing even between hard rocks. Their life force can compel them to grow in unexpected places, but they cannot grow well if they aren't nurtured. Sometimes they gets crippled and unhappy and cannot grow much. But other times, their small, persistent strength may move the rock out of their way.

"That is exactly the fate of human Selves when they encounter the world outside. They must follow their agenda. So, yes, there is a plot, but the course of this plot is not predictable, because we don't know how interaction with the world changes its course. It is the greatest drama in the world."

After the Self had watched the image with fascination, it became serious again. "Now I have looked inside me, but I still do not really know what is happening. What is all this movement, all this color, and all these changes? What is happening inside of me?"

"I will try to explain you to yourself, but there are several things I must say to you first. We really, really do not know who you are, or where you come from, or where you are going. We don't really understand our Selves or what life is. It is a mystery, and this fact is hard to accept. Humankind has developed many theories about you and believes they are facts, but in the end, all we can see is your behavior, your reactions to the world around you, and the world's reaction to you."

"Then we must find out who I am," said the Self. "We know that many Selves are suffering, not being seen or heard, and trouble results from that. They must have some help. There are also others who are flourishing, and good things are happening. How can we understand it all?"

"Should we play detective?" I asked.

"Yes, but use your own tools to find out." Suddenly, the Self was taking the lead. "Do not test me. Just use your powers of empathy, and observe me lovingly and trust your own experience."

"I also need my thinking tools, not only my emotions," I said. "Together, they are part of my ability to observe and form an image. I must construct a working model, something I can use to focus people's attention on you, to allow you to be seen, even though you are invisible. You must always remember, however, that this is only a simplified version of you, for we cannot truly fathom you."

"Alright," the Self said, getting impatient. "Let's look at the picture again."

"You see there are many things going on," I said. "This is an image of the mature Self. Later we will talk about how you grow. The purpose of all the commotion is to preserve your integrity and to allow you to grow and connect with the outside and fulfill your destiny.

"The big dark pool is the unconscious; it is the lowest layer of the model. It has several tasks. It is like a reservoir that contains everything that flows into it—biological information such as DNA, forgotten memories, experiences too painful to be felt consciously, drives, instincts, repressions, and much else. It is the unconscious that we are most apt to overlook, and yet it is often the missing clue to our actions.

"Let me try to explain. We have automatic reactions to stress or danger. We feel anxiety, passion, jealousy, the whole range of emotions. We do not know where these feelings and reactions originate, but they influence us. They rise from the unconscious into consciousness. You can see that happening in the picture.

"Then there is also movement in the other direction. Experiences crowd each other out. Some get pushed into forgetting. Some can be recalled at will. Then there are those that serve no purpose. Also, there are experiences or feelings that we rather wish we did not have, so we put them away in the unconscious. We may feel their presence as discomfort, even pain or depression.

"For example, when his new baby brother is born, Johnny has a variety of contradictory feelings—excitement at the new event, fear of being replaced, interest in exploring this new being, concern about how it will impact his life. Most of this goes on in his unconscious; some of it he knows. He feels a great need to be good. He does not want to displease his parents. He fears the baby will take his place. He feels real love and real jealousy. He wants to kiss the baby and also hurt it. His feelings are ambivalent. He devises a solution. He puts at least a part of the jealousy into the unconscious. Through this mechanism, he can even change it into the opposite, an over-abundance of love.

"But the unconscious may sneak up on him. His love seems so great that he squeezes the baby too hard. So his jealousy surfaces behind his back. Putting feelings into the unconscious helps us solve many problems in life that are too difficult to deal with. However, as in this case, they often do not disappear, but rather appear in altered form.

"I believe, however, that this is a necessary function. We could not live without it. There are certain things that are relieved if we can put them away temporarily, such as our fear of death. Putting it away helps the Self to function.

"The unconscious can serve as a Self-saving function, but it can work against the Self, too. This is especially true if it must keep certain feelings hidden, thereby keeping them from developing, growing, and changing. When a feeling hides in the unconscious, its absence creates a sense of emptiness where the feeling was before. It still has a hold on us, but because it is unconscious, we cannot deal with it. This can happen with events that are so all-encompassing that the Self would disintegrate if it had to face them. It sometimes takes decades before it is safe for the memories to reappear in consciousness. Only then can we look at them and integrate them into the Self safely.

"For instance, many refugees from the Holocaust are only now able to look at that terrible experience and try to emotionally digest it. That is why there are so many books being published today, and that is why so much dialogue is taking place now. The Self kept it in abeyance until it was safe to look at it. In the meantime, it took up a space in the survivors' unconscious and found an unexpected expression in other sorts of suffering, such as depression, illness, or anxiety.

"The next layer of the model is the subconscious. The subconscious exists between the unconscious and the conscious. Feelings can move in and out of it; it is where things can be temporarily put away. While we are concentrating on a task, such as driving a car, we forget our worry about a sick child, but we can pull the feeling back out at will.

"The next layer is consciousness—a very complex part of the Self—which keeps interacting with the unconscious and the subconscious. It exists as a buffer between you, the Self, and the outside world. It is like a watchdog.

"Freud developed three concepts: id, ego, and superego. They are a useful model; however, I would be wary of any preconceived notions of what these mean. The id, for example, carries a particularly negative connotation, but I see it differently. My model includes no value judgments. I see the id (or let me call it a driving force) as that which includes our passions, our needs— really our life force. It is the passionate love we all carry: love of our mother, a sexual partner, a spouse. It is also the drive to accomplish a task, to learn, to attack or desire. The id is not, in itself, positive or negative, but rather it is a strong impulse toward its own expression—an expression which may clash with the environment, with some of our needs, or with another's needs. It is an energy we need to regulate in order to live with each other.

"It is the ego that takes on the task of regulating the id. It puts on the brakes, so to speak; it deflects; it redirects. It regulates the relationship between the inner and the outer world. It is aware of both worlds, and as the child grows, the ego develops knowledge and sophistication. It learns about relationships; it learns about dangers. If you go near the neighbor's dog, the dog might bite. So the ego tells you to control your desire to pet him. A little girl sees her father across the street talking to the neighbor. She gets excited and filled with love and wants to run into his arms. But the ego, which has incorporated the voice of the mother, says, 'Don't follow your desire to hug your dad because a car might come and run over you.' The little girl suppresses or postpones her desire to run because she listens to the inner voice. The ego knows both the inner passions and the voice of reason."

The Self looked at me questioningly and said, "So the task of the ego is to bridge the expectations of the outside world and my needs?"

"Yes," I said. "It is a safeguard to protect you. The ego has many functions, all of which serve to protect the Self from outer and inner harm, and to support its necessary expression. It might be the factor that puts certain experiences into the unconscious.

"Another domain of the psyche is the superego, the conscience. This is where the moral and ethical values exist after they have developed. It is also where guilt feelings are at home."

The Self looked dubious. "Does the superego have a purpose? Where does it come from?"

"It also originates from several sources and has a number of purposes. It exists both in the unconscious and consciousness. The superego internalizes some of the expectations of society. It insists that we don't break the rules and laws that parents and communities impose on us. It is another very important way in which we integrate our inner need with outer expectations. It is what makes us feel guilty if we steal or tell a lie.

"There is also direct input from your basic life force. You feel a connection with nature, with others. There is built-in empathy or altruism that even makes us want to sacrifice some of our needs for our children or parents, our spouses, friends, and our fellow human beings. In fact, their needs become our needs, and so we can put them first and let go of some of our own needs."

The Self became thoughtful. "I think I can understand this. It seems that there is much movement between these different areas— between the unconscious, subconscious, and consciousness; between the id, the ego, and the superego."

"Yes," I said. "That is part of your complexity; it is the flitting around and changing which you see in the picture."

"But how does this movement occur? What makes it happen?" asked the Self.

"That is a very good question. Actually, it happens in a number of ways. Anna Freud and others call some of these 'mechanisms of defense.' These are means that you have developed to defend against being overpowered by emotions. Defense mechanisms are just one of the ways that you manage your relationship with the environment in order to grow without restriction or injuries. They allow you either to incorporate and add something to your inner agenda or to put the impulse away temporarily or permanently."

The Self said, "You are going to have to explain this better. This is just gobbledy-gook to me."

I started thinking about finding a way of explaining some of the mechanisms. "Let's assume that there is a bully who is waiting for us at the corner. He has beaten us up many times. We feel anger, fear, helplessness, hatred, and unfair treatment. Our first impulse might be to hit him back as hard as we can and really hurt him. But we know that would be too dangerous. Also, our parents have told us that fighting is not a good way of settling things."

"But," said the Self, "we are so filled with these feelings, how do we get rid of them?"

"So what would you do?" I asked the Self. "Here you are, filled with wrath. What could you do so you will not be so helpless or so you will not do something that is dangerous?"

"Well," it said, "I could maybe dream about it. Yes," it said, warming up to the task, "I could pretend all of the terrible things I want to do to him. I could even pretend how it feels to do it. I could play with my toy soldiers and shoot him and, and, and...."

"So, you figured out one way. Pretending could help."

"Absolutely," it said. "But then, our mother does not believe in war toys."

I answered, "We might have to talk about that another time. Let's first figure out how you, the Self, can protect yourself against being overwhelmed by your emotions."

"Alright, I will wait with this question," said the Self.

"You just proposed one mechanism of defense: substitution. You substituted fighting with pretending to fight. It took some of the pressure off, even though it did not change the situation."

"No," the Self continued, "and it didn't change my feelings. I am still angry and scared."

"So," I said, "what else can you do?"

"Well," said the Self, "I could do more thinking about it."

"That is right," I said. "There is another mechanism called sublimation. You are replacing action with thinking. Sublimation leads to real growth for you. We replace a behavior that is not acceptable in society with one that gives us the same satisfaction. A good example is how the impulse to express anger by hitting or biting can be changed into verbal expression. The use of swear words serves this purpose and can get further sublimated into solving conflicts by talking about the problem. Since all through life our inner agenda meets with the outer agenda, there are always occasions for conflict between these two. Sublimation can play a big role in integrating the inner and outer agendas without injuring you."

"That makes sense," said the Self. "But what would happen if I could not use sublimation or another approach?"

"There would be no way to reduce the anger or pain. Can you imagine what would happen?"

The Self looked frightened. "I would be so filled with anger, I might really try to kill the bully."

"That's right," I said. "Some people who murder other people are those who have built up too much anger but have not developed the means for control."

"But then," said the Self, "that is what punishment is for."

"But," I asked, "How would you feel if you were told only that you would be severely punished if you were to hurt the bully?"

"I would still have the feelings."

I could see how the Self suffered merely from the thought of it. "I think I might explode and do something terrible."

"That's right," I said, "and that is why you need to develop the ability to sublimate."

"Are there other ways in which I can sublimate some feelings that are hard to deal with?" asked the Self.

"There are many, and I probably cannot enumerate them all. One of them is denial. When I described before how Holocaust survivors put away the pain, I was describing how some of them denied its existence. Denial can help us cope with something of such great magnitude that it is really impossible to cope with. However, at some point, we will need to look at it, for it comes out in other ways, as I described before.

"Another method is projection—expressing feelings in a situation that might be less dangerous for you, the Self. For example, a man's job is often the basis of his financial security. He is afraid to tell his boss how humiliated he feels by the way he is being treated. So he goes home and screams at his wife for some minor irritation. All the accumulated feelings against the boss, the deep hurt to the Self, are expressed so that the anger against his wife is grossly exaggerated. He really screams at his boss in the guise of his wife. This type of projection might relieve some inner pressure, but it often brings new pressures with it.

"Projection appears in many ways. Anything we are afraid to handle directly is a breeding place for projection. This happens especially where there is a difference in power. Children are often innocent victims of an adult's anger that the adult cannot express in other, more dangerous situations. Adults project feelings onto children, children onto adults, and children onto other children. Here is an example: A little girl is frightened of her teacher, who is most loving. It turns out that the teacher looks just like a woman who took care of her when her mother was in the hospital and who the girl did not like. The child obviously has projected her feelings about the caretaker onto her teacher.

"The purpose of this and all of the many complex structures inside you is to ensure your healthy growth and protection."

"Well, how do I grow in a healthy manner?" asked the Self, obviously wearying of this whole construction.

"Before we answer this question," I continued, "We need to determine at what point after conception the separate Self appears. We don't know the answer, but probably rather early, in the mother's body. There is a protected place where a separate Self begins to grow, along with its separate physical body. Much growth and change and actual living happens before birth takes place.

"I will now tell you how I feel the healthy Self grows and also what can go wrong. When a child is born, the impact of the outside world is overwhelming. The emerging Self cannot face this world alone. It needs the lifeline of relationships with caring adults. These relationships form the protective hallway of growth. The delicate balance between the inner and outer world is mediated by empathic interactions with the primary caretaker. You, the Self, on your journey, encounter the needs, world views, and agendas of other psyches. The nature of this interaction with the primary caretaker determines much of the growth and development of the Self. At birth, the emergent Self bursts into this world with enormous passion, needs, and desires. The strength of these passions, which comes directly from the unconscious, will impact the interaction between the Self and the world.

"Deep inside, don't we often feel ourselves to be tiny and powerless, confronting the mysterious and often dangerous outside world? How do we manage this awesome task? The tiny Self cannot do it alone. You, the Self, need help to face this challenge."

"Well," it said, "it looks like an awesome task. How do I get the help?"

"The prototype for all encounters with the outer world begins at the moment of birth, and in some ways, it stays with us throughout life—you, the Self, with your inner agenda, confronting the complex world with all its contradictions of danger as well as support.

"Help is available in the form of the parent or parent substitute, who re-establishes some of the safety and comfort felt in the womb by giving physical nourishment and care and cuddly love and comfort. Soon that love is reciprocated with passion. The whole universe exists in this motherly hug. All our lives we long for this net of safety.

"The relationship to the mother or caretaker is the prototype of all relationships. It is truly our lifeline—an invisible replacement for the umbilical cord. All future relationships are modeled after this primary one. That is why relationships are the basis of all emotional, intellectual, and even physical growth. This relationship expands to others in the environment, and to the family unit, the first community that becomes the prototype for future communities that also become a part of the inner safety net."

The Self paid close attention. It said, "Just listening to you, I feel overwhelmed by having to live in this exciting and frightening world. How do I manage to cope with this confrontation?"

"The answer to this question lies in the original relationship. To consider your question fully, I want to discuss the care and maintenance of the original relationship, the importance of the basic lifeline, the impact it has on you and your inner agenda, and in fact, how you feel about your Self. The fact is, we learn to love ourselves based on the original bond to our parent.

"Your unconscious hope is unconditional acceptance and love from your all-powerful parent, gradually expanding to the world. Realistically, it is impossible for your parent, who has other connections that go beyond you, to provide you with this. In other words, your parents' own conscious and unconscious needs impact their vital bond with you. On a continuum, the more uncluttered with other factors the relationship remains between your parents and you, the freer you will be to blossom.

"This original relationship is the basis of your trust. Within this framework, your inner agenda grows and develops as you learn to differentiate and increasingly recognize your own environment. As your primary relationship develops, you come to possess some inner control and become capable of confronting your chaotic internal and external worlds without panicking. Throughout your development, the parental relationship is a lifeline that creates the possibility of growth through the development of sublimation and other vehicles for inner transformation.

"On the other hand, if this relationship is flawed or if the outside demands are too great, panic sets in. I have seen panic reactions in young children. A positive experience with the primary caregiver teaches trust and overcomes panic. Where the relationship is flawed, the Self internalizes the panic. When this happens, it becomes more difficult to develop the inner structure of control and mastery. For example, two young children have to have an appendectomy. One parent arranges to stay overnight in the hospital with one of the children, even though she must occasionally leave to take care of other responsibilities, and the relationship is an honest, open, and secure one for the child. This child has been told the truth about the operation, and he is prepared for what will happen. The other child has had a conflicted relationship with the parent, was deceived about the severity of the operation, and is left alone in the hospital. A feeling of abandonment overcomes her. She feels that she was a bad girl and is being punished. There is great panic. Her Self feels terribly threatened."

"What does she do next?" the Self asked.

"She takes her crayons and writes all over the walls in the hospital. She cannot control her anger and anxiety. Now she has a reason to be punished. Had she had a trust relationship with her parents, she would not have felt abandoned or that she was a bad girl that should be punished. She would have known how to wait for the parent to return and provide comfort and reassurance."

"I see," the Self said. "It was safe for the first child to wait; he has learned to postpone gratification."

"Yes," I replied. "The Self learns inner control when it begins to realize that postponement means soon—not never. When postponement is learned safely, the Self accepts adult power as supporting its needs. As time goes on, the ego begins to regulate between the needs of the child's life force and the outside world. The intellectual ability to differentiate self from other increases. The Self receives more and more satisfaction as it masters eating, love, play, sound, light, discoveries. Within this lifeline relationship, growth takes place without fear. In the usual course of events, the Self grows along with the body, developing power, control, self-expression, and creativity, while learning to adapt and to submit. The ego also learns to regulate the demands made by the environment as the Self tries to follow the demands of the parent and incorporate them into its own world. The goal is to find one's niche in this world and make one's impact on it, while understanding that time and attention must be shared. The Self learns this best if a trust relationship is established. That is why all children need emotional allies and advocates."

"And how does this happen?" asked the Self.

"The parental lifeline continues as the parent endows the Self with the continuity of the trusted relationship. Following the parent, the teacher has the sacred responsibility of maintaining the child's psychic equilibrium as he or she enters the new world of the class-room. This new phase opens the possibilities not only for the contin-ued flowering of the child's Self, but also for unintended injuries by the conflicting needs of the adult's and the child's psyches. In this new stage in the child's growth, the world of the Self expands into peer relationships, object relationships, and mastery of the structure of the world. If this place is not safe, the Self must fight for survival.

The transition to school represents a step into the world away from home. It is another new beginning, another experience, which will become a prototype for the future. This is particularly important for the Self of the gifted, which is characterized by a greater awareness about the mystery of life and a very strong inner agenda. We must try to envision the high drama between you and the outside world. Little David, the Self, is confronted with Goliath, the expectations of society."

"Will they integrate, or will it be a struggle?" the Self asked.

"This is the big question," I responded. "The integration of these two forces is the goal of the Self and should be included in the goals of education and society. If the merger is successful, the Self can blossom, form, and create.

"The young Self needs the interaction, confirmation, respect, and stimulation from the outside world. The outside and inside belong together. Together, they orchestrate the symphony of life."

And now the Self spoke strongly, empowered by its new understanding of its inner being. "I now know that I am powerful and that there are billions of Selves like me in the world. We have the power to destroy or make it the wonderful place it is meant to be. We, young Selves, need all the help we can get. Please learn all you can about us and treat us with respect and love, for the fate of the world depends on us."

The Red Flash

The inner dialogue between the different parts of the Self is taking place in all human beings. Some of it is conscious and verbal, and much of it is unconscious and nonverbal. If we watch ourselves, we can see that we spend more time negotiating, arguing, consoling, deceiving, and exciting ourselves than anybody else. So it was not surprising when, after a rather long outward silence, there was another knock on the inner door of the "I." This time, it was a loud, impatient knock, and my inner door flew open before I could even say, "Come in." There was the Self, breathing hard.

"What is happening?" I asked.

The Self replied, "I need your help. Since we have been born, from time to time I have been getting these flashes penetrating me. They are painful; they say, 'Watch out!'"

The Self got red and agitated and continued, "They say 'DANGER' in big flaming red letters. I feel attacked. It makes me feel I have to defend my Self. I get angry. I get nervous. I get frightened."

"What might bring this on?" I asked. "Is it one of the inner dialogues that we have with each other?"

"It can be so many, many different things. It can come from the inside or the outside. Here is an example: When we were young, our mother sometimes did not listen to us because she was busy with the baby, so we started running around the room to get her attention. We felt a pain inside of us. We needed her attention. Since the baby was born, there had been many red flashes and danger signals. We felt that something was disappearing below our feet. We felt that our mother didn't see us anymore. Something powerful that had been giving us confidence was disappearing. We were afraid that the bond with our mother might not be there anymore. To make sure she still knew we were there and she still loved us, to make sure our mother still belonged to us, we began to do many things to get her attention. All this was because of the red flashes, which were actually the outward expression of our fear of losing her love. Another example: When we were four, our father said, 'I know you can ride this bicycle,' and a flash of danger went through us. We were afraid to try, but more afraid to disappoint him. It felt so heavy inside. Or when we were six and the teacher said, 'Why can't you focus?' Again, a flash of danger went through us. We already knew how to read, and it was so boring. What will happen if we don't focus? What is all that focusing stuff about anyway?"

I told the Self, "In all of these situations, it feels like a state of emergency has been declared. In situations like this, it feels like you must defend yourself against something, but you are not sure what it is. It is such a feeling of discomfort."

"Yes, yes," the Self said. "It disrupts everything. It can make us sick to our stomach and feel like throwing up. Even thinking about it makes us feel bad."

"I think the red flash has a strong effect on us," I said. "It makes us forget what we already know, like how to spell or drive a car. It makes us fight, thinking it is Self defense."

"It makes everything look kind of slanted, out of balance. Why do we have this disruptive experience? Is there a reason?"

"Yes," I said. "It is really a warning signal. It says, 'Watch out,' and it keeps you from stumbling or crossing the street without looking both ways."

"So it is both good and bad for us. But it happens so much, and it really interferes."

"I have a thought," I said. "Maybe we can learn more about it and make it help us rather than interfere."

At first, all I got in response was a faraway look.

"The image of a red flash is related to, but somewhat different than, stress," I continued. "It is a sudden pain, a shock, a push; it penetrates. The red flash is the reaction you have the moment you see that the car is going to hit you, the moment you feel that the one you love loves someone else more. The red flash distorts, at least temporarily, your view of life. Maybe we could introduce the red flash as a concept in the vocabulary. For instance, when we try to evaluate or understand a child or an adult, we might ask, 'Is there a red flash involved?'"

"Oh yes," said the Self. "Remember when we saw little Jared, and you knew his father *needed* him to be gifted? And even though we do not test, we could tell he was so afraid of failure anyway, because he felt that his dad's love depended on his success? I remember watching you, and I saw that you avoided anything that looked like an evaluation, and it still felt dangerous to him. So there was interference from the red flash."

"Every human being feels these flashes of danger, sometimes several times a day. We can observe it in animals, as well. Animals seem to feel these danger signals sooner and almost in a deeper way than we feel them. Strangely, we seem to take it for granted that the rats leave the sinking ship or that cats and dogs get restless when an earthquake or other natural danger is about to occur.

"In the last few years, many have come to believe that gifted children have expanded senses, such as better hearing and better vision, and they react to both inner and outer circumstances more strongly. They will sense when red flashes hit their parents. The flashes feel to the soul as a sting with a needle to the body. At any moment, whether concentrating on a task at hand or contemplating inner thoughts and images, you may be stopped with that red flash. We can feel it in ourselves, but if we are observant, we can notice it in others. It immediately changes the inner situation; it adds a new factor.

"Much of human activity, in our hierarchical structures, consists of testing and evaluating in the belief that we can find out a person's abilities and characteristics. Given that being tested is often highly stressful, it is possible that the answers we get are dominated by red flash experiences, and the very characteristics we are looking for may be the ones that are missed by a test. Children are particularly subject to red flashes. It is harder for them to judge the extent of the danger. Also, they feel their own lack of power to keep things from happening. They feel their dependence on adults. Dependence in itself often creates danger signals in children if they are not sure whether the adults will react in terms of the child's needs or their own, for these two sets of needs might be quite contradictory. One of the frequent causes of the red flash in children is when they feel threatened by adults. This could be through the tone of the adults' voice or their actual words. Sometimes a child will pull his courage together and say, for instance, to his father, 'It scares me when you yell at me.'

"It is at such moments that children feel invaded by the sudden red flash of fear. Then they often feel paralyzed in their reactions. Daily in school they are expected to prove something. Being continually exposed to the burden of proof often burdens the child with an ongoing stress. The red flash becomes stress when it continues to inhabit our soul for a longer period. Here is an example: A father I knew asked his son three questions every day in order to make sure that the son would be prepared in the event he got lost. The questions were: What is your name? How old are you? Where do you live? The child knew the answers perfectly well and answered the questions correctly when his mother asked him, but he was so afraid of his father that the red flash appeared and grew into a full-fledged examination anxiety, which almost kept him from graduating high school. Interestingly, if the bond between caregiver and child is well-established and the child feels protected in a cocoon of love and security, the red flash doesn't happen so often.

"Many adults are plagued by red flashes when their childhood experience did not allow them to secure their inner Self. They did not internalize the parental support and therefore are not really able to function on their own. They have to use devices and rituals to protect their injured Self.

"Many different sorts of events can bring on red flashes, and it is often unpredictable which sorts of events will cause people anxiety. For example, there was a woman who was convinced that her neighbors talked about her all the time, and every little remark became a red flash for her. However, in carrying and delivering her two children, she experienced no anxiety. Three days after she gave birth to her children, she was back at home worrying that the neighbors might come over and see what a mess the house was.

"This red flash reaction is one of our many mechanisms designed to alert the Self, but it has the capacity to become self-defeating. It is an important and often overlooked factor in the well-being of the Self. When a Self is suffering, it is useful to inquire about what the red flashes are inside."

The Emotional World Wide Web

There is an extensive network of nonverbal communication among the Selves of the world. It is like a huge spiderweb that transports knowledge, feelings, and experiences everywhere. Most of it is unconscious and uncontrollable by our conscious mind. When one observes people and their reactions to each other, one can find that spoken language is among the least important components of the communication that is happening all the time. Facial expression, body posture, tone of voice, and movements all convey meaning and are received in a place of accumulated experiences and meaning. People have, of course, always been aware of these communications, but because we did not believe in the existence of the Self or the unconscious, we did not listen to these communications or trust them. Now, some even believe that they not only exist between beings that are near each other but can travel around the world and crisscross it in amazing patterns. We are also becoming aware that it happens among animals, and between people and animals, and actually between the occurrences in our surrounding and all living things. In the past, all we knew were half-believed stories. The telephone is busy because two people try to call each other at the same time. A friend appears prominently in a young boy's dream: the friend looks at him, turns around, and walks away. The next day, the boy gets the news: the friend has died.

Once we begin to believe in this mutual connectedness, we realize that we sense each other's emotional reactions. We sense the feelings but not the thoughts, so we can't really tell what it is that makes us feel uncomfortable at some moments and good at others. We can't really read other people's minds and thoughts; we can only feel the energy and the vibes that come from another person. We may be able to translate some of it into words, but mostly it's a transfer of energy and emotions. In other words, a person may come in with a terrified expression after a frightening experience. What we can see is the terror, but not the story behind it. This is a very important insight, for we also have a tendency to guess what the occurrence might have been and then impose our own interpretation on it, which may or may not be appropriate.

Often, there are whole chains of connections that transport emotions from one person to another.[5] For example, a mother and daughter became ill with anorexia. When the daughter was five, she overheard someone say that she was the only thing keeping her anorexic mother alive. Nobody realized at the time how deeply she took the remark to heart and how she accepted responsibility for her mother's life. This child learned all about the disease and studied her mother closely. She began to have symptoms, much to the surprise of the doctors, and by age 12, she also had a full-blown case of anorexia. Mother and daughter had a symbiotic relationship: what one felt, the other felt also. The child became identified with her mother to the extent that it seemed they had one soul. One could almost say they had a joint pathological experience. When I met the girl, her arms were thin as sticks. My task became helping her understand that she was not responsible for her mother and needed to have a Self of her own. This needed to be handled slowly and carefully and was only possible because she developed a very trusting relationship with me. At the same time, her mother worked with another therapist who slowly worked in the same direction. It was a very delicate and long process, because I had to consider the deep sensitivities which prompted this child to take her unusual course of action. When the daughter understood that she was not responsible for her mother's health, she quickly improved. The need for inner separation also sped her mother's recovery. The mutual love and dependency, which had led to joint illness, became the emotional engine that led to joint recovery.

Positive Manipulation

Donna, age seven or eight, was sent to me through a social worker who did not know how to help her. She was so bright that she had mastered all of the skills that we painstakingly try to teach children; her language was so sophisticated that a truly mutual relationship with other children was virtually impossible. The social worker was counseling with the child and the whole family. I worked with her for several years and was able to establish a rapport with her. It meant so much to her that she finally found someone who was emotionally on the same wavelength. I could accept her feelings for what they were without pathologizing them.

Donna's main problem was that she was very lonely and could not find an appropriate place for herself in her environment. Her loneliness and resulting unhappiness expressed itself through a number of nervous habits. One of them was chewing her shirt and sleeves so that they were always wet. Because she was so highly gifted and her language so much more sophisticated than that of other children, they couldn't understand her, and she therefore had no friends.

Because of her difficulties in making friends, Donna became concerned about her own normalcy. In my work with her, I was able to help her realize that there was nothing wrong with her; she was simply in a different place than other children. We tried enrolling her in the only school for gifted children in her area. The school turned her down because of her chewing habits, deciding that she was too nervous. We were then able to work out a program with the public schools which she could tolerate. The school gave her advanced work; she went to school only until noon; and for the afternoon, her mother secured a job for her in an electronics shop where she could use some of her knowledge and skills in a very concrete way. Instead of being seen as a problem, she became acknowledged for who she was.

At that point, I felt that Donna did not need me anymore and that we should discontinue our sessions, but she insisted on seeing me once a week, and it became a puzzle to me why she wouldn't let go. My only clue was an intuition that I had. I felt more and more strongly that in some way, her clinging to me had more to do with her mother than with herself. I felt that she had a concern about her mother that she needed me to help her with. When I finally decided to talk to the mother about it, the result was sudden and unexpected. This mother broke into inconsolable tears and said that she did carry a heavy burden about which she had never spoken to anyone but her husband. It was always oppressing her. After her own father's death, her uncle had started sexually abusing her at the age of five, and it had continued for many years. There had been no way for her to tell anybody about it, and she had suffered with its legacy for the many years since. After she told me this, I recommended that she get therapy for abuse victims. She did that, and her daughter relaxed and had no further interest in seeing me. It is noteworthy that Donna never knew that I spoke to her mother, nor what her mother's problem was, but a wave of relief settled over both of them. All of this points to a great deal of unconscious communication among all of us: the mother, the daughter, and myself. The last I heard of Donna was that she had gone to college at a very young age.

One could say that the girl manipulated both her mother and me in a positive way. Donna had an unconscious goal to help her mother and was able to achieve it by continuing her sessions with me until I approached her mother. It confirms my belief that the traffic between souls has a large place in our lives. Intuitions such as the one Donna had are probably more common than we realize, but they are rarely allowed to surface. They can be a burden to a child who is sensitive and intuitive. It might even be said that children connect with the past, with trees, animals, and stones. They are driven by these mysterious connections and an accompanying sense of responsibility. Our deepest passions drive this web of connections: passions of love, of hate, and of fear. We do not know where the energy of passion originates, but we know it reaches other people.

I believe that all beings have these mysterious connections with each other and with unknown sources. They are available in the beginning of life. The adult world typically does not believe these experiences or ignores them; it even places a taboo on speaking about them. As a result, children are driven to push them into their unconscious or to keep them to themselves. There are occasions when they come back to consciousness, and there are those people for whom they have not disappeared.

Chapter 2

The Birth of the Self

The birth of a child is a mystery and a miracle that is repeated daily over the globe. In fact, birth is many mysteries: the fact of creation and life itself, the ways in which all newborns are similar, and most of all, the infinite variety of body, mind, and Self so evident in each new miracle of birth.

This endless variety repeats itself wherever we look in nature. Just watch the unfolding of the flowers as they grow in rich earth. Each exhibits a unique beauty that is increased manifold by the beauty of their combined uniqueness. All human beings hold inside them the mysteries of personal growth. I pondered this awe-inspiring wealth when I saw a photo exhibit by Sebastico Salgado, a South American artist. He took pictures of children all over the world. In each picture, the child's eyes look straight at you. Standing in the exhibit, it was as if you were standing in the middle of 50 faces of children—shown in a variety of situations and often at full stature—looking at you from all directions. It felt as though each picture had been taken with great care and loving acceptance. The artist seemed to have understood the innermost individuality—the Self—of each one of these children. I felt exposed to such depths of emotion and such an amazing wealth of knowledge. It became a very humbling and overwhelming experience, almost a sacred event. It made me imagine that I was the recipient of hundreds of secrets without ever knowing what they were.

In every newborn, we are surprised and awed by the complete-ness of the human being. The tiny eyes look out at the world from a miniature body that is poised to grow into the adult it is destined to be. Along with the body, another equally astounding mystery is born: the Self, that which feels and reacts and is the tiny "I." It, too, is already complete and very complex and ready to grow into its des-tiny. All the senses that connect to the world outside are there: the beginnings of passions, love, and all of the other feelings we are capa-ble of experiencing. All of these emotions are ready to grow and be nurtured. The tiny Self is not contained in itself, but it stretches toward the outside world, which is just as mysterious as the Self.

Our Self at birth begins to separate from the mother's Self, just as the body does, and to cope with the fate that awaits it. This Self is also ready to grow. There is an emotional hunger just as strong as the physical one. This hunger is the desire to live and learn and love and create, to fulfill one's destiny, to be protected, and to be loved. Love is the emotional nourishment needed for existence. After World War II, children who lost their parents were placed in orphanages. The orphanages were understaffed, and the turnover of personnel was frequent. Consequently, the babies received very little human touch or sustained attention. As a result, they did not thrive; they stopped growing, got sick, and many died. This tragic trend was partially reversed when the caretakers were told to be more affectionate toward the babies and to cuddle them several times a day. The nour-ishment of the emotions is as important as physical nourishment.

A newborn child is emotionally and physically not yet able to face the world by herself. Just as in the womb the tiny being is nur-tured by the physical umbilical cord, after birth there is an equally necessary emotional umbilical cord that provides the emotional life-line. The experience of birth is an enormous physical and emotional trauma. We are pushed out through this narrow channel to confront the unknown: glaring light and noise and smells and touch and taste. Everything that is familiar disappears into one dizzying experience. At that moment, the baby's first skills are also born: to reach out, cry, and get attention. This crying is an expression of desperate need. If help does not come, the helplessness is overwhelming. Crying babies are truly unhappy.

The Task of Developing Emotional Trust

The task of both adult and child at this point is to develop the emotional trust and emotional skills, along with the physical skills, that give the child some control over his vulnerability and an element of power. Developing his initial trust and bond of love is the basis of emotional growth. For some children, it takes a few months before they develop any type of emotional and physical comfort and trust. These I believe are not the colicky babies, but the gifted. They are physically and emotionally extremely sensitive. They are the ones who cannot stand wet diapers or anything else that touches their delicate body and soul. They are the ones whose drive for survival forces them to begin to develop their ability to judge their surroundings in terms of inner and outer safety or dangers. They develop their strategies and defenses early. These infants gauge the intentions of their surroundings. The unconscious questions they ask of others is: Are their intentions honorable in terms of my emotional and physical survival? Am I safe with those on whom I totally depend? The ability of these babies to make these assessments grows as they grow, and the process comes ever closer to consciousness. Their gaze tries to penetrate to our very souls, and we cannot hide our true motivation from them.[6]

From the moment of birth, the reception that the newborn receives in the world initiates an inner dramatic dance, filled with great energy, passion, beauty, and also desperation between the two Selves who are now separate. The Selves of both parent and child learn to become familiar with each other and to keep the flow open through the invisible umbilical cord.

Here is a poignant example: As a baby girl, Ratasha remained inconsolable no matter what the family did. Advice abounded: put her on a schedule, let her cry it out, don't let the baby control you. The mother felt early on that this child was quivering with sensitivity and the desire to be recognized. The mother knew instinctively that these were legitimate needs and decided to trust her inner voice. She discovered that holding her daughter calmed her down. She moved out of the house for a few weeks with the baby and held her constantly. Women in many cultures know the importance of holding their babies and always carry them on their backs. After a few weeks, Ratasha seemed to begin to trust her mother and quieted down.

The child's distress is not caused by the parent's shortcomings but by the child's deep craving for love and security. It takes time to build trust in the child. When trust has been achieved and continues to be honored, the invisible umbilical cord will nurture the growth and learning.

Some of these children will be truly angry at their helplessness and will never stop screaming. The child's rebellion against his helplessness must be allowed to play itself out. My experience with many highly gifted children tells me that their exquisite sensitivity is probably present pre-birth. I believe that the sense of rootlessness, disconnectedness, and abandonment at birth is overpowering. Much is asked of parents of such children. If the parents' efforts are not immediately effective, they tend to feel guilty and frustrated with their own inability to help the child. They need to understand that they are not doing anything wrong. They can rest assured that if the right energy is transmitted through their emotional umbilical cord, these children will find ways to protect and soothe themselves. As these children grow, they typically develop the emotional skills to cope with their own sensitivity.

It is not, however, an easy process. The trust issue is more difficult for gifted children. They need emotional space to allow trust to grow. Each time a child begins to walk, an act of great courage has taken place: "I can trust this physical and emotional ground to keep me safe. I can trust my own power to act independently. I can trust my environment to catch me should I fall." Children with heightened emotional sensitivity will have a harder time accomplishing this step.

An illustration: A little boy did not attempt to walk or become actively involved in life around him, although there were many indications that he was well aware of his environment. His family was concerned that he might be retarded. He did not walk until about age three, and he was late to start talking. Later, to the great surprise of his family, a test revealed that he had an IQ of 180. Once this fact was known and help was available, this boy's talents became increasingly clear. He simply delayed taking his first steps until he felt sure he could do it competently.

Michael

Michael is another child for whom the entrance into this life was difficult. It took him a long time to develop trust. He cried for the first six weeks of his life, sometimes for 12 hours at a stretch. No one could find any physical reason for his distress. His parents felt that he was particularly sensitive to all physical discomfort, such as wet diapers. He seemed to feel total helplessness. Being thrust out from a small, warm, protected, familiar inner space into the cold, limitless, unknown world was too much for him. He must have felt like a rudderless boat, adrift and out of control, yet assailed by new experiences. He must have craved some solid support.

His parents met these complex reactions with empathy and understanding. They knew what to do without the help of example or experience. They were poised to be open to his needs. The invisible umbilical cord provided the necessary guidance. He would only quiet down when he could lie on his father's body, feeling warm, safe, and solidly supported. Slowly, parents and child became acquainted with each other, finding ways to communicate. Michael learned to trust that he did not have to face this world alone. As he grew, they mutually learned to consider each other's needs. The parents surrounded him with a cocoon of love. It allowed him and his family to trust his inner life. When his younger brother was born two years later, Michael welcomed him with a minimum of jealousy, for he didn't feel threatened, not even by the brilliance of his brother.

Paula

Paula, too, had a rough beginning. Her father left her mother, who had health problems. As a consequence of the divorce, her mother became destitute. After birth, Paula cried continually and needed to be held and carried constantly. Miraculously, her mother managed to hold and carry her while taking care of everything else as well, all on her own. Early on, her mother recognized that Paula had developed health problems. The doctors did not believe her until they ran the proper tests. Her mother struggled alone to give her baby all she could. In this way, Paula had a secure emotional lifeline.

School was a problem, too. At first, Paula had trouble learning and was far behind the others. Even though she had periods of depression, she remained cheerful with a strong underlying sense of Self, for the emotional lifeline was open and the trust was always there. Slowly, but with increasing speed, she caught up with her peers in reading and other areas. She was talented in drawing cartoons, which were original and well-executed. They earned the respect of other children and her teachers.

Paula took pride in being different. She found a way to express her creativity and to maintain and increase her self-esteem. She created an inner world of fantasy and realized her facility in drawing cartoons. She knew that she wanted to make this her lifework. When she talked to me, I was impressed by how well she understood her goals and ambitions. She was very articulate and mature in her views. She understood what she needed to do to overcome her difficulties, and she did overcome them.

Paula was clearly gifted; her mother's original support had opened the road to her Self and the world. She was aware of the differences between herself and others. She told me, "I am different, not one of the cool kids. They are phony." A natural drive and mysterious strength seemed to come somehow from the depth of her being. Her mother had kept the channels open through the lifeline that exists between them. She helped this strength develop more. In cases like this, the Self seems to have mysterious connections that grow if supported by trust and love. This was not just a sentimental experience, but real energy that flowed between those two.

Gustav

There are mysterious connections that sustain and develop a Self's growth without the support of a parent, too. Gustav was found at a street corner, aged about 10 days. When I met him at three years old, I was struck by his deep, knowing, curious eyes. His face had something of a universal expression. If I ever saw an "old soul," he was one. As a rule, I see a child alone for one session, but this time, his adoptive mother stayed in the room, which felt right to me. Gustav looked around the room, playing halfheartedly with the toys. He answered my questions but otherwise would not really talk to me for half an hour. Then he started to draw and gave me a look that seemed to say I had passed muster. He smiled a little, then talked a little. I admired his adult expressions and command of language. He gave me the strong impression that he was his own person.

While most children derive their confidence and personal strength from the bond with their parents, in Gustav's case, the bond with his adoptive mother appeared to have been formed from the strength of this child's own Self. The bond was clearly strong, but his strength seemed to flow as much from the inside. When he was doing his drawing, he worked with complete concentration and total confidence. The only moment of concern was when he saw my rather scary, long, green stuffed snake with its tongue hanging out. As I watched him, I could see that he had a certain fear and that it interfered with his inner safety. His mother asked if he was afraid of the snake. He said, "Yes." The mother asked, "Is it real?" to which Gustav replied, "Yes." He gave it to his mother to hold, then he playfully attacked it with my puppets (butterflies, ants, June bugs), pulling the snake's tongue and giggling all the time. It was clear that he worked with the same concentration on overcoming his fear as he did on his drawing. Then his mother asked, "Now, do you still think it's a real snake?" "No," he said, "it's not."

Gustav had found a method of mastering his own emotions and coping with them. He looked at his fear of the snake and at whether or not the snake was real and, in his way, investigated the situation, arriving at the conclusion that the snake was not real and therefore presented no danger. In this way, he was developing his own curriculum of growth of the Self. A curriculum of emotional growth is necessary for the development of the Self, and we need to include it in our thinking about children.

Chapter 3

The Curriculum of Growth of the Self

The Curriculum of Growth of the Self grows, in part, out of the encounter between the Self and the world. Birth itself is the first encounter—and it's a David and Goliath experience. Imagine the drama of this tiny Self confronting the enormous world and demanding a place in it! The task is overwhelming and can only be accomplished with help from the powerful beings—the adults—around her. The love that radiates from the parents to the child becomes a powerful cocoon, within which the Curriculum of Growth of the Self begins to develop.

Almost every day, the child's body and Self learn new skills. They are driven to learn. They have to try out everything, to put everything in their mouths at first, to learn to crawl, and to make certain noises. Their bodies are learning and growing all the time, and their Selves grow right along with them. The emotional growth is just as built into the psyche as physical growth is built into the body. Each new skill adds to the expansion of the Self. The child crawls, stands, and finally walks. The same milestones happen emotionally: emotional crawling, emotional standing, emotional walking. The ability to walk grounds us to the earth emotionally as well as physically. It brings us closer to feeling at home on this Earth. It is as though the Self is saying, "I belong here now."

We could look at learning to walk as the first emotional graduation of the Self. Anybody who has watched a child take his or her
first steps can't help but feel what an enormous accomplishment it is.
I wouldn't be surprised if some children were actually conscious of
the great emotional accomplishment of their first steps. Here is an
example from personal experience: One beautiful, sunny Sunday
morning, our family was sitting outdoors at the breakfast table. Our
one-year-old daughter was dressed in her Sunday best, and my husband George had the movie camera in his hand. Our daughter was
on the ground, playing with a toy, when she pulled herself up on the
table leg, looked at George, spread out her arms, and started walking. Of course, her first steps were recorded in the family movie.
She's been a dancer ever since.

As they grow, children are exposed to impressions and sometimes interference from the outside, and the Self grows or stops
growing in response to every experience. Often, the feelings, which
develop during all this time, seem much greater than the small body
they inhabit. When the Self feels endangered from the outside, as
with an illness, or on the inside, as with the experience of a lack of
ongoing love and attention, great anger can appear. A furious child is
like a winter storm! The power of their fury, if experienced by a sensitive soul, can be terrifying. A furious baby is literally convulsed
with feeling!

The Self becomes a kaleidoscope of different emotions. As the
healthy soul grows, the desire to learn takes on many differentiated
extensions. At the same time, the need for self-protection is always
present, and it can be an obstacle to the natural growth. The goal of
the Self is mastery over the pressing needs from the inside as well as
the expectations from the outside. Much can get lost on the treacher-
ous road that the soul has to travel in order to accomplish its growth.
If it has the protection of love, the tiny soul won't need to hinder its
growth with doubts and anger. The desire to explore this wonderful
world will continue, unfettered, and by the time children reach the
age of four, more or less, they know who they are and feel a kind of
ownership of their world.

This inner life grows from the Self, which changes and grows as it interacts with the outside world. Every experience adds something to the growth or causes a change in the Self, even though we may forget it soon after it happens. These changes continue all through life, and growth can happen until death. As the Self grows older, there are habits of the soul which express themselves in habits of behavior, and these habits are often a necessary form of self-protection.

The world of fantasy is most instrumental in developing the Curriculum of Growth of the Self—and who truly knows where the lines are between reality and fantasy? The internal world that children create is real, peopled with angels and fairies, kings and princes, animals who speak, supermen who fly, and all of the fictional characters in the modern child's world, as well as those of children of ages past. It expresses itself in the stories, drawings, and dancings of children, and it speaks of their great drive to understand our world.

The gifted child whose fantasy life dominates his daily living and growth is also the one who has a sense of the geography of the earth; who is learning how to read, write, and do math; whose factual knowledge surprises the adults around him; and who delights us and himself with his amazing wisdom and insight. This may be the child who spends hours playing *Dungeons and Dragons*™ (a fantasy game), who knows all the characters of *Pokemon*™ and *Yu-gi-oh*™. Images of the unknown world, life, and death develop right along with reading, writing, and arithmetic. We need to stop making a distinction between our sense of reality and theirs.

The Curriculum of Growth of the Self is the expansion of self-actualization. It allows feelings to be seen as real, and as the Self grows, emotions become more intricate and expansive. Love, for which we have no adequate definition, is probably the original emotion. In the uninterrupted Curriculum of Growth, it begins with Self-love, moves to love of a parent, to love of a playmate, to love of other growing Selves, and to grownup Selves. It moves from sexual desires to the different phases of sexuality. It also moves to love of humankind as a whole. We may also move from one lifetime to another and from one reality to another—some form of love probably includes it all.

The drive to experience this world creates the desire to learn, to discover, to explore. It is what has brought us to our present state of knowledge. Yet because we have no language for emotions, our emotional maturity lags behind our intellect. Sigmund and Anna Freud have given us a basis from which we can put the Curriculum of Growth of the Self into an understandable framework. Substitution, sublimation, projection, and denial: these are the names that Freud has given to what I call the Curriculum of Growth of the Self.

One of the first skills children learn is substitution. Babies learns to substitute one way of fulfilling their needs for another. A baby cries and, when no one comes right away, discovers that when he puts his thumb in his mouth, he feels a temporary satisfaction. For a while, his need to eat and suck is satisfied. If his nourishment appears in the form of his mother's breast, he feels the delight of the warm milk entering his body, and in the meantime, he has learned a skill: to substitute. From then on, emotional learning follows the physical learning. He learns to hold somebody's hand and gets security from that. Each time, his Self becomes more secure in this world. All through life, we substitute unattainable goals with attainable ones, and they help us adjust. Children who are allowed to play with water and clay will toilet train more easily, because they learn to substitute playing with water for the sensation of wetting themselves. When three-year-old Dillan hits Carlos and is told by the teacher that this is unacceptable, the next time he may stop and say to Carlos, "You're a dummy!" Unfortunately, parents don't always realize that this constitutes progress!

Sublimation is another mechanism, one that gifted children use when they expand the love for the parent into a love for mankind. One psychoanalyst said that the gifted replace love for the parent with love for the world.

Another skill children learn is projection. A child will transfer some of her feelings from her mother, who may be away from home, to the babysitter or a teacher, with whom she spends many hours every day. Generally, if a child feels that she can rely on the emotional support of her mother, she will also trust the babysitter or the teacher. The feelings are transferred from one to the other, and this transference means emotional growth because it expands the area of trust relationships.

A very important skill that helps us cope with the tragedies of the world is denial or suppression. These allow us to deal with a tragedy or trauma by not fully emotionally experiencing it. Being a refugee from Germany myself, I've watched with awe many people who had to start their lives all over again, in the U.S. or somewhere else, after experiencing the tragedy of Nazi Germany, concentration camps, and the loss of family members. The individual stories of healthy survival are heroic testimonials to the emotional strength of the human Self. The way these people found to cope with this enormous emotional burden was to learn to deny the emotional impact of the experience at the time and, as we found out later, postpone feeling it to a time when it could be better incorporated into their psychic lives. The many books that have come out in the last 20 years about the life experiences of victims of the Nazis are a testament to this.

My own experience is so totally clear in my mind today—as though it were a painting. I was forced to leave my parents' school together with my father. At the moment of departure, I felt that I could not experience the separation and told myself to stop the feeling. I remember how successful I was. I denied the unbearable emotions of separation from the happy days of my youth. This resulted in the fact that I suppressed most of my feelings and felt I was not existing until I was reborn at 21 in the United States, when I began my fruitful and successful life here.

My visits to Germany after that were those of a foreigner visiting another country. Around the time that my husband died in 1992, my feelings began to melt. On one trip to Germany, I felt for the first time the full pain of having left it and could connect a little more to my early life experiences. In the summer of 2004, I went back to visit our German school, Marienau. I received a very warm reception, and for the first time, people there expressed their sadness about what had happened to us. It was only then that I felt a reconnection with my earlier life, as when two parts of a train come back together, and my life seemed to be whole again.

For children to develop these psychological mechanisms, they must first feel unconditional love and acceptance. It is only through this bond that we can help them to learn and grow. The basis of any learning is a relationship between teacher and child and subject matter. When Selves have gone through many of these stages of growth without losing their emotional ability to grow, they almost invariably become people with a sense of justice who understand their interdependence with the rest of the world. We must understand that learning takes place from the inside out. We must replace strategies and intervention with relationships and empathy. I am hoping that we can learn that the process of education would profit from including the inner curriculum.

Chapter 4

The Growing Self and Its Continuing Encounter with the World: The Evolution of the Curriculum of Growth of the Self and its Expression in Social Action

As a child grows, the Self of the child and the world around it stretch more and more feelers toward each other. These become mutual relationships, each of which emerges slowly into the child's personal environment. These relationships are formed with everything that comes the child's way, whether it is objects or people. The Self of today's child is confronted by enormously sophisticated technological structures, which totally defeat me, while young children grow the emotional and cognitive capacity to control them and use them at will. This ability of the human mind and Self is amazing to behold, because it seems to grow along with the increasing exposure to technology.

I've observed with great fascination how young children master modern technological inventions. The two-year-old who knows how to insert a DVD into the DVD player, a task that I have only barely learned, gains a sense of mastery, which adds to his curriculum of the inner self. He now possesses that valuable skill. He also learns how to express his love for his mother through a tender hug. Both times, his Self has grown, but the growth is different in each case.

Indeed, the most complex emotional, cognitive, and spiritual relationship is the one to another human being, both within the family structure and in wider circles of contact. These relationships begin with the home and the family and slowly spread beyond them. Soon the Self becomes a crowded world of feelings and emotions. The necessary stabilizing factor is the relationship to the person the child is closest to, usually one of the parents. For the gifted child, all of this is experienced against the background of expanded awareness and sensitivities.

From the day a child is born, there are two strands of emotional growth, both intertwined and in opposition to each other. One drives to understand and conquer the world and to find a place in it, and the other reacts to the pressures that come from the world outside. The dichotomy between these two strands expresses itself prominently in the relationship between the goals of education and those of the Self. Since these goals are often divergent, the parents become the pivotal element between school and child. The process of education occurs in the interaction of these three agents: school, child, and parents. If the interaction functions well, the child's Self is free to grow and blossom. If the three agents turn against each other, the child's emotional energy is channeled toward survival instead of growth. Often, it becomes the child's sole task to maintain that precarious balance.

The Self finds many routes to integrate into society's expectations, which are most often represented by the school. Starting school becomes for many children either an entry into a new world or a struggle to maintain their own agenda in the face of overpowering demands. It seems to me that children are forced to make an uncomfortable choice between these two alternatives.

Until recently, children were trained to look upon their own Self as something negative, something that stood in the way of the outside agenda of socialization. They often saw the expression of their own life force as a hindrance. This is true to some degree for most children whose inner needs do not coincide with those of society. For the gifted child, it is even more poignant. Children, especially gifted children, are often chided for being impulsive, making impulsiveness something to be overcome.

I interviewed a highly gifted nine-year-old girl who had decided on her own that she wanted to see me (most children are brought to me by their parents). When I asked her why she felt the need to see me, she said, "You might be able to help me because I'm too impulsive." I asked her, "Is it wrong to be impulsive?" "Yes, my teacher said that's my problem. I act before I think, and that's bad." This child reacted passionately to anything that came her way. She could be extremely happy or extremely unhappy, and she felt that her passions needed to be suppressed. She was surprised when I pointed out to her that an impulse is not necessarily a bad thing. If you saw a two-year-old child run into the street, would you call it an impulse if you tried to save him, maybe even without thinking of your own safety? This is an example of how children's direct expression of emotion has often been suppressed.

Almost everything that school is about involves the suppression of children's natural emotions, of the basic integrity of the Self. This creates an environment where the Self feels humiliated and offended by the daily denial of the worth of the child's own agenda. Unless a child can feel the support of her parents, the loneliness of this Self who feels misunderstood and degraded is almost impossible to describe.

The Self is the energy center of the person. I believe Carl Rogers was probably right when he said that in its essence, the energy of the Self is always positive. The negative and destructive actions that a person feels compelled to take are always the result of suppression and injury to the Self. Many gifted adults have told me how, as children, they felt constantly insulted by the lack of acknowledgment of their deeply feeling and insightful Selves. When a child is exposed to many such insults, he is forced to believe them to be true. As a result, the child's sense of Self becomes stunted.

The healthy reaction of the Self when it is attacked is to defend itself. When this happens, the child feels driven to do things that go counter to the rules. This, then, creates a new kind of pressure for educators who feel they need to modify the child's behavior so it will conform. In cases in which a child and the school do not find common ground, the support of a child's parents can make all the difference.

Here is an example: Nathan was feeling misunderstood by his highly regimented school. By the time it became clear that this was not the proper place for him, it was too late to change the arrangements. But as soon as Nathan knew that his parents understood that this was the wrong school for him, he felt a great relief. He was able to wait out the year with less stress, as he knew he was going to transfer to another school the following year. Today, many parents and educators are learning how to support the spontaneity and natural vitality of children by showing them support and understanding.

No matter how well a child feels supported by his parents, and often even when the school makes great accommodation, if there is a large gap between a child's own direction and that of other children, it can become necessary to find a way to bridge the gap. In the absence of some corrective measures, the child can feel too isolated. Just like adults, children need some sort of meaningful contact with others. Often, children unconsciously look for some sort of bridge to connect them.

This was true for a highly gifted six-year-old girl I once saw. Her parents were highly gifted themselves, and this family formed a little community in themselves, a world apart from everybody else. None of them was able to sustain a relationship outside of their closed circle. The parents may have formed a thin connection to the world through their work, but they were deeply isolated in a world they only shared with their child. Even so, they tried to help her to make a connection within her classroom. This child felt the need to be like other children, but the only way she knew how to do it was by creating a pretend person. Because she was so different from others, she had no way of knowing where and how she could fit in. Yet she found it meaningful to play with children, so she figured out how other children did it and created her own activities and pretend play that were understandable to others. Her means of adapting were not completely successful because the gap was so great.

With play figures, this girl created an imitation of school and organized a pretend world quite strictly. Her play was very intellectual. When she came to see me, she gave me a performance of her play school. She created an imitation of ordinary children. It was beautiful but cold. I guessed that it served to defend her against loneliness.

In her sessions with me, she was reserved. Our roles seemed reversed, as though she was evaluating me, and I got the impression that I didn't pass the mark! I got the feeling that she was more gifted than most children I know. There wasn't any other child in her class who came close to measuring up. She had developed a way in which she could communicate with children and adults, yet she felt out of place in the classroom and in the world. She had learned to fit, but she hadn't really found herself. I don't believe that her mother understood who this child was—nobody did, not even the little girl herself. She had concluded that in order to live in this world, you have to behave in a certain way. She was simply behaving in the way that others expect and using the play school game to gain access to other people. She wasn't particularly interested in letting me know who she was. This was a child who remained hidden. I believe that this should be respected. She should be allowed to remain hidden until she feels ready to make herself known. It might be that she will recognize her own depth when someone enters her life who has a deep, intuitive understanding of her essence and her life agenda, or the emergence of her Self might come about in its own unique way.

Every Self has an inner agenda that drives the individual. Gifted children have a stronger inner agenda than non-gifted children. When any child's inner agenda is interrupted, disregarded, or denied, conflict emerges. This happens when the child is no longer permitted to do what he feels an inner imperative to do. Instead, the outside world demands that he behave in certain ways. Adults may get aggravated and ask him to be more obedient. But we must realize that he *is* being obedient—he is just obeying a much stronger force within himself.

Disobeying this force would mean the destruction of the Self. The Self lives by different rules and has different expectations than those on which we base the conduct of our affairs. Therefore, there are many occasions when Self and society are strangers to each other, with contradictory interests, values, and imperatives.

I would like to use the learning and teaching of math as an example of certain difficulties that arise between schools and gifted children, and how these issues then result in procrastination. I've seen enough of this type of friction to realize it is a common occurrence. Gifted children are often concept learners rather than skill learners, and the world of mathematics is most exciting for many of them. They feel compelled to try to solve the mysteries of the world. Many of them will penetrate very deeply and understand things in very different ways from most children and even adults. They have an intuitive way—or at least a way that we don't understand—of solving math problems. Teachers, however, want proof and will not accept an answer without knowing how it has been arrived at. Teachers pressure children to prove their conclusions, and they demand that the gifted child suffer the daily grind of homework, producing many examples of the same thing.

Erica, age 11, was extremely gifted in math (she was solving mathematical problems of her own devising before knowing algebra), science, and computers, as well as literature, history and psychology. She was endowed with a wonderful sense of humor. Her mother was very supportive of her gifts; mother and daughter delighted in solving mathematical and scientific problems together, and they would seek new problems to solve. Intellectual activity was a pastime, and this allowed Erica's mind to expand, her knowledge to advance, and her emotions to grow. Her mother did not make demands, but together they explored the world of mathematics, science, literature, and the arts.

In contrast to this free-flowing collaboration and exploration, the school that Erica went to was "infamous for its heavy homework load." Erica began to procrastinate under the burden of an overwhelming amount of homework. But because she was also a perfectionist, it was nearly impossible for her to cope with the assignments. One day she told me, "No matter what I finish, the homework never ends!"

Erica was in severe distress from the pressure in school. When she began to explain to me her difficulties, she wanted to know if I thought that gifted children have problems because the subject is boring or whether there is some difference between their desires and the subject. With this question, she zeroed in on the heart of the matter. "It's not that it's really boring, but it's not exactly what I'm looking for." Her greatest need was to share with me her inner turmoil. Sharing an inner conflict is almost more of a relief than solving the conflict. It is this process which is important in relating to gifted children (as well as all other human beings). When we try to help each other, we almost always feel that we must try to solve the problem, when in reality, the more important need is to understand the problem.

After Erica had shared her problem with me, we were able to talk seriously about her procrastination. She said that she couldn't bring herself to do what she had to do. I pointed out that procrastination is a complex feeling: it combines anger, anxiety, frustration, and all sorts of other emotions. We arrived at an image for this: education feels like a one-way street where you are not given a choice. Then you come to some sort of crossroads, with the school's expectations on one road and your inner agenda on the other. Erica said that this was almost right, but not exactly. We were involved in a deep process, trying to understand each other.

Then I asked her whether she knew where the pressure came from. She said her parents were not the source of the pressure, but that it came from the school, where grades were put before exploration. Erica felt she had no way out, hence the procrastination. She had come under such conflicting pressures that she was paralyzed. Much as she tried, she could not go against her inner agenda, but neither could she ignore the pressure from the school. Her anguish over this communicated itself to me in a most palpable way. At home, she felt free, but in school, she felt constrained and unable to perform because her inner resistance was so great.

Preschool used to be a place where children were free to play and learn through play. More recently, learning to follow instructions, submission to order, and restrictions on free movement have become the rule. The irony is that while parents are feeling freer to support their children, schools are becoming more rigid and demanding. In one preschool, children were observed listening to a tape giving detailed instructions on how to sit still, when to pick up a pencil, and when to apply it to paper. This early insistence on learning to follow the rules is perhaps the reason for a trend in the formation of new charter schools.

Children themselves are acutely aware of the ongoing trend toward more restriction. One four-year-old boy, who complained to his parents about the lack of freedom in his school, said to them, "It's not the teachers, it's the administration." This remark in itself reveals the close connection between parents and children which makes the children feel supported and free.

Many parents are now seeing their child's schooling in a different way. Instead of taking for granted that the system is immovable, they are beginning to see that it needs to bend to the child. Parents are seeing that schools can be obstacles to true learning and growth, and rather than insisting on conformity and acquiescing to the school system, they are supporting their children in seeking accommodations that are appropriate for their child. Parents are starting to understand their own place and importance in the partnership between the school, the child, and themselves. While they are learning that the child cannot help but express his own inner drive, they are also learning that the same is true for themselves. The system has had both children and parents in bondage. Parents have measured themselves and their children against the expectations of the educational system. They are developing a new set of expectations that frees their Selves, as well as those of their children.

This new attitude of both parents and children has led to a change of behavior in school. Since parents are not pushing their children into submission to the school, struggles between the school on the one hand and both parents and children on the other are becoming increasingly common.

When he was in sixth grade, Regulus went to the principal and told him he was leaving the school. Then he told his parents what he had done. How had this happened? Regulus had been attending a good private school, well-meaning and friendly to children. There were 12 children in his class. He was a leader and did well. But by the time he was in sixth grade, a curious reversal began to happen in which he had become a behavior problem for the teachers and was frequently punished. Teachers began to pathologize his behavior and suggested that there were something wrong with him emotionally. When I saw him, he was upset and sobbing. "I am a failure," he said. "I would rather not be smart and have problems."

To heal, Regulus had to stop assuming that the teachers were right in their point of view and realize that he had rights and that his inner reality was as valid, or even more valid, than their reality. Thankfully, standing up for himself was in keeping with his extended family of mavericks, artists, inventors, and sailors. He gradually gained inner strength and realized his power. His reason for leaving the school was that he felt guilty that his parents were spending money on a school where he was not learning anymore. It was a victory for his Self. His parents understood, accepted, and supported him in this.

When he left the school, Regulus's greatest wish was to learn circus tricks. He found out that there was a circus school nearby that trains children. After dropping out of his school, he finished the school year at the circus school and enrolled in a different type of school the following year.

Regulus is a clear example of a child supported by his family in pursuing his own agenda. When there was a disconnect between the school and the child, at a certain point, the child outdistanced the school, and the school was no longer able to meet his hunger for learning. The school became a hindrance, but fortunately, the parents were on the side of the child.

Today, parents are more accepting of the children's wisdom than in the past. A three-year-old girl listened to her mother on the phone talking about her. Rather than misbehaving to get her off the phone, the girl waited until the mother finished, and then told her, "It doesn't feel good when you talk about me, because it's my life, not yours." The mother accepted this. The child understood that she had rights as a person and felt free to express it. This is an important departure from the way young children usually understand their own position in the world. This child knew she was in charge of her destiny, but she also understood her dependency on her parents and their superior experience. Most importantly, she understood that it was their goal to support her.

When I met Sunan, he was about eight years old and showed the expanded sensitivity that I have seen in so many children. He had a feeling for what was going on in the world and experienced it honestly. He felt the problems of the world with emotions like sadness, anger, and fear. This resulted in his having difficult times. He wrote beautiful poetry about the state of the world, about life and death, about the unknown beauty of the universe. He experienced it all very deeply and went through many emotional upheavals. But the greatest upheaval for him was that other children neither understood him nor shared his concerns. At school, he felt isolated. For several years, he tried to emulate others so that he would be popular, but he nonetheless felt like an outsider. When I met him, it was in a social situation, not a formal evaluation. He immediately started talking to me, telling me about a new discovery he had just made or maybe a new decision he had come to. What he said to me spoke volumes about the growth he was doing. "All of a sudden I realized that I don't have to be like the other children," he said. "I must just be true to myself and not hide my poems from them, but let them know what they are, and they can decide." After that, he went to a different school, one that understood him better, and came through the experience endowed with this new wisdom about himself.

I remember a number of other children who, when they were young, went through very insecure times. They all seem to have felt that other children knew better and that they had better imitate others. Some of them would hang on to the other children and be with them all the time; others would try to imitate their behavior. But there would inevitably come a time—it might be the beginning of adolescence—when they came into their own. One little girl had a very hard time in nursery school. She hung on to another child and had a hard time finding her own way. Then, when she returned from a trip at the age of 12 or 13, she showed that she had found herself and was ready to take charge of her path. She realized that she really was a leader, and at the age of 15, she became involved in social action for the first time, organizing a bunch of other children her age to bring over two children from Yugoslavia during a difficult period. Her task involved fundraising, traveling, and making arrangements with schools and foster parents, and she has been involved in social action of this kind ever since.

It is most important for these children to be actively involved in bringing about social change. I believe this allows them to become happy and satisfied. When they are very young, they feel they need to do something but don't yet have the power to do it. As they grow, they gain this power and should be encouraged to utilize it to engage the world in constructive ways. It is more important for their growth and contentment to allow children to carry out social action than to be forced to do their homework.

It does, however, take these children some time. If we followed one of them over time, we would find that the child who comes crying and screaming into this world may all of a sudden develop a strong Self, realize an ability to lead others, and follow a desire to change the world.

Gertrude Weiner before her marriage to Max Bondy

Max and Gertrude Bondy, circa 1917 during World War I. Max, who like many Jews was a patriotic German, had volunteered and was on a visit from the Front.

Annemarie, age 2, and her mother

*Above: Gertrude Weiner Bondy
(Annemarie's mother) with Annemarie
(age 7) on left, sister Ulla (age 3) on right,
and brother Heinz (age 1) in pram*

*Right: Annemarie's father, Max Bondy,
circa 1940*

Below: Annemarie's sister, Ulla, about age 18

Marienau School located near Dahlenburg 100 km southeast of Hamburg. The little pond in front of the school, where Annemarie paddled her canoe, plays an important role in the life of the school. It was used for boating and ice skating, and much activity takes place near the shore of the pond even today.

Right: Annemarie at age 16

Below: Annemarie, about age 16, and friend Hannele Baruschke at a restaurant near the Elbe River

Above right: Student jazz band in the main house at Marienau. Music was part of the daily rhythm of the school. Each morning started with a Bach fugue and was frequently followed by singing at meals and some kind of musical or theatre performance in the evening.

Right: Entrance of the main house at Marienau School. The room above the main entrance was Annemarie's bedroom.

Below: Students building the soccer field at Marienau, circa 1932. The school house is in the background.

Above left: Max Bondy, circa 1929, with a typical expression. He was very protective of his few remaining hairs, a subject of many jokes.

Above right: Leaving Germany in 1937, fleeing the happy places of childhood. Annemarie is in the background to the right behind her father.

Below: Annemarie and her husband George in Atlantic City, October 1940. The beginning of married life, which lasted more than 50 years.

Annemarie teaching at the Roeper School in Bloomfield Hills, Michigan, circa 1970.

Left: Annemarie and George, circa 1968

Right: Circle time at Roeper School. Many discussions and teaching at Roeper School occur in an informal manner such as this gathering.

Bottom: Hill House at The Roeper School, founded in 1941

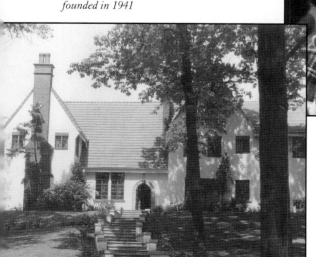

Above left: George Roeper receiving honorary Ed. D. degree in 1978 from Eastern Michigan University.

Above right: Annemarie Roeper receiving an honorary degree from Eastern Michigan University in 1978.

Below: Annemarie speaking in Germany, circa 1978.

Left: Roeper School graduation ceremonies.
Annemare is wearing a necklace made by her cousin,
George Lauer, after he retired as a chemist.

Annemarie and George Roeper after the Oakland Hills
firestorm of 1991.

Global Awareness meeting at Annemarie's house, circa 2004.
Back row: Maddi Wallach, Patricia Gatto-Walden, Betty Meckstroth, Ellen Fiedler,
Noreen Ward. Front row: Linda Silverman, Annemarie Roeper, Michele Kane.

Chapter 5

Relationships and the Self

A newborn Self is but a slice of the universal mystery. It simultaneously becomes a unit in itself while remaining part of the "All." It is the separated consciousness—the slice—that struggles to find a connection to an earthly reality. This struggle has its origin in the fact that we can only find our own identity—we only feel real—if someone else or even something else lets us know that we exist. Only then can we believe in our own existence. Love is the longing to be united with other human beings. For most, there is a primary relationship with another, but we also possess an inner community of relationships within us. Sometimes these relationships are with an object or even a mission. All relationships, both inner and outer, ground us to the here and now, tie us to this Earth. It is the power of relationships that makes it possible for us to develop emotional roots and grow.

Relationships become the little trestle around which the Self winds itself and hold on and grows. There is usually a primary relationship, one that we need for any kind of inner safety. Any motivation for learning and growth stems from this primary love. Without it, there is no motivation for growth, and if that motivation gets derailed, it can lead the Self to resort to destructive behavior.

The invisible bonds and communication that form our relationships can be found everywhere. When they are cut off, however, we find ourselves lost and floundering. Bonding and communicating most often begin with the parent, but they could equally begin with a nanny, a grandparent, a sibling, a teacher, or a school bus driver. It is generally assumed that parents feel responsible for their children and feel the obligation to take care of them, but it is not generally known how frequently the reverse is true. Children have a very strong basic need to protect their parents.

Sometimes children recognize their own strength when faced with the weakness of their parents. Alexis, a sensitive little four-year-old girl, was riding with her mother in a car through a snow-storm. The car slid a number of times. The mother, feeling out of control, became terribly frightened. Alexis became aware of her mother's fear and said, "Move over, Mommy, I'll drive." The need to protect her mother and to relieve her was so great that the child felt the strength to meet the challenge, even though her plan of action far outstripped her actual abilities.

A mother and her three-year-old daughter, Sarah, were alone in the house during a terrible storm. The mother suffered from a phobia of storms; she was so frightened that she was shaking with fear. Sarah was aware of this and was overcome with sympathy for her mother. "Mommy, come sit on my lap," she said, and the mother actually put her head into the child's lap and felt comforted by Sarah stroking her hair and speaking soothing words to her. By being protective of her and holding her, the child helped the mother cope with the storm.

In some cases, children are so intuitive and so altruistic that they take on a challenge that is beyond their capacity. Here is an illustration: A five-year-old boy came into my office bent over, and acting on a hunch, I said to him, "You look like you carry the burden of the whole world on your back." "But I do," he replied. "Every-thing goes wrong at my house when I don't watch out." His seven-year-old sister had a bad illness, and he said, "I need to watch her because my mother is too anxious. And besides, I have ESP." I asked him how he knew. "On the way here, I thought I was going to see an accident, and I did see an accident."

I worked with him for several years. Things became more difficult for him because his mother felt overwhelmed by her daughter's illness and the boy's precocity. There was nothing to correct for his belief that everything rested on him and he had to be in charge. He felt that he had nothing to learn from anybody and that he should make the decisions. He began to create bedlam: he did not listen to the babysitter, his parents, or his teachers. His father was a military man but was not highly respected by his wife or children. I felt that something had to be changed in the basic familial constellation.

This is one of the situations that sometimes arises in families with gifted children wherein the familial constellation is reversed and the child becomes the leader. In reality, this boy was in no position to take this role and wanted somebody to stop him. He didn't want to carry the burden of being in charge, and he needed protection. I felt that his acting out was a cry for help. "Stop me," he seemed to be saying. I realized that the crucial person in this situation was the mother, and that I couldn't help the child without strengthening her belief in herself and her position in the family.

At the same time that I began to work with the mother, the boy was sent to Roeper School, where the situation itself taught him that he was not in charge and that there were others equally bright. As a consequence of his changed self-perception and of his mother's stronger self, the situation seemed to resolve itself. Unfortunately, the father was transferred to another state, and when I last heard from them, things had taken a turn for the worse. The boy was no longer in a school that was appropriate for him, and the mother had lost my support.

This was a case in which the child's advanced ability to sense the family situation did not match his emotional capacity. Like many gifted children, this boy overestimated his obligation to rectify the situation and suffered greatly from the demands he put on himself.

Adults have the power to disrupt a child's relationships, and this can cause profound pain. A boy, Akim, and his half-sister, Natasha, had a very close primary relationship. It was through each other that they felt real and were able to grow emotionally. But Natasha lived with her mother and an older sister. The parents kept rearranging the schedule for their time together. The children had no reliable pattern of knowing when they would see each other again. Both children were increasingly overcome with the pain of frequent and irregular separation. Each separation created a deep sense of loss in them. The scene was repeated so many times that the children began to show signs of stress. They became nervous and tense. Akim had trouble sleeping, and Natasha withdrew more and more into her own private world.

The three adults could not agree on what was best for the children. The children had to try and cope with all of this by themselves. The adults failed to see that for Natasha and Akim, their relationship with each other was the primary one and needed to be considered in all of the planning and scheduling. The interactions between the children and adults became a wild and chaotic landscape of conflicting emotional messages.

Failed relationships are among the most painful experiences anyone can have. Unfortunately for gifted children, their relationships are typically more fragile than most, and their sense of exclusion can run deep. Relationships with peers are often tenuous, especially when gifted children are concerned. The loneliness and sense of rejection a gifted child may experience can have a major impact on the development of the Self.

"I feel invisible. I am invisible. Recess is the worst time," said David. "I feel I don't exist. I cannot stand it. That is why and how I get into trouble. The other children just walk around me." David described how he stretched out his foot. Another child tripped on it and swore at him. David knew he existed for a moment. But he still felt that he did not belong. Emotional loneliness, even more than physical isolation, is the truest deprivation. Children suffer deeply from it, and it can explain a child's need to share a parent's bed. The need for the adult at bedtime is most serious for young children.

Relationships are the most important mutual support that exists between people, but they can also be the most destructive force. They can be both health-giving and illness-creating. It is through relationships that we define our reality. "I am loved, therefore I am," might be a truer statement than, "I think, therefore I am." Young children have to check in with their mother every once in a while. They have to make sure they are still loved, and then they can go back to their pursuits.

These other pursuits can, themselves, be quite absorbing. "Keisha cannot pay attention in class." Labeling her with ADD would totally miss the point—she is forever trying to find out if Caitlin pays more attention to Sonja than to her; she feels lost without Caitlin. These children are confronted with a reality conflict. Their relationships cannot and should not be manipulated, but we should be aware of them and take them seriously. We help children by explaining to them how relationships work. More than anything, Keisha needs another relationship: one with a supportive adult.

In my 40 years as head of the Lower School at Roeper School, I spent the majority of my time and energy coping with the vast network of relationships that existed within the community of children, parents, teachers, and support staff. Sometimes the power and energy that these interactions released was heavily loaded with needs, anxieties, hopes, disappointments, and everything in between. These interactions, rather than classroom instruction, were what both my husband and I felt to be the centerpiece of the school community.

Chapter 6

Learning about an Expanded Reality from the Spiritually Gifted

When I first started working with gifted children, I knew exactly what the difference was between reality and fantasy. We lived in a real world—that which we couldn't see or touch or explain as fantasy. We did not even believe that feelings were real.[7] We were blind to anything that could not be understood concretely. We knew that the gifted had a rich fantasy life and, in fact, felt that we had an obligation to make sure that they knew the limits of what was real and what was not.

Over the years, however, the gifted have taught me that it is not so simple, and I have begun to see our daily experiences from the perspective of these spiritual children. Slowly, I began to include more and more experiences in my reality.

The more I truly listened to children—hearing their expressions and watching their amazement—the more I could detect their spiritual knowledge and their otherworldly experiences. This is how I came to understand that our concept of reality is much too limited. The limits of what is real expanded for me as I learned about the expanded senses of gifted children. I realized that they can hear things most of us can't hear, see things most of us can't see, and that a touch to their skin is felt more strongly than most of us experience. I realized, too, that much of what I had taken for fantasy was very much reality.

It was after this realization that I had a true inner discovery—namely, that reality is not absolute, that even reality, as Einstein says, is relative. The physical reality and the physical laws under which we exist are known to us as immutable, and our minds have difficulty comprehending deviations from this reality. Yet when I included relativity in my thinking about reality, I began to realize the true meaning behind much of what I heard from gifted children. I am truly grateful to my many experiences with highly gifted children for these insights. They have taught me the difficult fact that reality is relative.

Interestingly enough, even though each Self is entirely different, certain themes seem to repeat themselves in the way they express their spirituality. Many gifted children, for example, have a fascination with small rock collections. They often brought them to their sessions with me. I could never understand what this fascination was until one day when I asked a child, and he gave me a very clear explanation: "These rocks are alive. They are alive just like the Earth is alive, and," he said, "I can feel it." At that moment, I truly understood what he was talking about. His was an expanded experience of reality. He not only understood that all rocks are alive, but that the Earth has a spirit of its own and that everything is connected.

On that same day, I had a very interesting experience which seemed spiritually connected to the rock collection of the child. A picture arrived at my house, sent by a teacher from Roeper School. It was a woodblock print of a famous Japanese stone garden that serves as a place for meditation. The picture had belonged to my husband George, who had grown up in Japan. We had forgotten it when we retired from the Roeper School. It was his favorite, and we had not known where we had left it. To me, there was a spiritual connection between these occurrences. In fact, I wasn't really surprised when the picture appeared. The connection felt totally real. It revealed another insight: namely, even though we speak of a separate Self, we are spiritually connected to each other and the universe as a whole. It is my belief that this connection exists in everyone's unconscious, but that the gifted are uncovering more and more of these relationships because they know that reality is greater than that which we perceive in everyday life.[8]

This sensitivity and the understanding of expanded reality brings with it the need for self-protection, because the outside world does not understand and often interprets these behaviors as pathological. Sometimes when children seem to be in their own world, it's because they feel a need to retreat from the outside world. These children have to cope with both worlds, and they are not always in sync. Being so open to extended experiences can cause children to feel overloaded. We need to understand their unusual behavior in this light and must allow them their own way of reacting, even though it may seem strange. The child who won't take off his jacket and keeps his hood over his head may be trying to keep out the bombardment of other people's feelings and expectations. The child who needs to hum constantly may be expressing her inner tension. Much of what we interpret as negative or pathological is simply the expanded awareness that can result from giftedness. If their behavior becomes a disturbance in a classroom, it has to be dealt with, but it's important not to pathologize it. These children need to be accepted for who they are. We need to delight in their beautiful Self and to realize the enormous contribution they will make to mankind if they are allowed to bring their expanded reality to us freely, uninterrupted by our limited concepts. We must be sensitive to the needs of these children and their expanded sense of reality.

So how do we define reality in terms of the spiritually gifted child, who knows many things and experiences many things that the rest of us can't experience? While we certainly can't understand everything about it, we must accept the fact that the spiritually gifted child does not just live in unreality, but in an extended reality. If we can see it in this way, we will find ourselves interpreting this child's behavior quite differently.

Thoughts on Spirituality

Spirituality means different things to different people. For me, it is the totally unbiased view of the unknown. For many people, it is represented by the word "God," and God, for them, actually means "good." Some are resistant to truly accepting the idea that we cannot truly know who we are, where we come from, where we're going, what creates our many feelings, what is life, and what is death. Many find this uncertainty so unacceptable because it creates an unbearable anxiety. To fend off this anxiety, some people continually insert some firm belief in place of uncertainty. They can believe that the universe is good, or that there are spirits protecting us, or the like. Many gifted children need to protect themselves with these sorts of beliefs, and they will talk about how they protect themselves, as though wearing pretend armor. Truly not knowing feels vulnerable, and many people feel that they need protection.

One powerful defense mechanism consists of making rigid categories of reality. The world may be divided between good and bad, heaven and hell; young children talk about, "good guys" and "bad guys" and invariably see themselves as the good guys, who are powerfully defeating the bad guys. It seems inevitable that some judgment insinuates itself between our acceptance of not knowing and our Selves. It's as if we can't really get away from some kind of judgment.

Some see a world peopled with people and spirits and ghosts and angels and devils and demons and fairies. It sometimes gives one the impression that the world of the unknown has become overcrowded with beings. This owes itself to the fact that we are incapable of accepting our not-knowing, just as we are incapable of comprehending infinity and eternity.

It's generally impossible for people to accept the fact that value judgment is totally rooted in our limited human experience. Amazingly enough, there are gifted children who can live with the knowledge of not knowing and include it with their view of the world. I remember a nine-year-old boy with whom I had a very deep conversation about this subject. He said, "The universe truly doesn't care about you one way or the other, and we just have to accept that." Praying for your daily bread is a concept rooted totally in this world. For this child, this was not a frightening thought. It made him unusual. The modern gifted child seems to be moving toward an acceptance of the unknowability of the universe.

Most of our hostility, anger, and aggression—which in turn lead to our cruelty and inhumanity—originate from our need to deny the nothingness that extends infinitely beyond the limited world of our experience. The more we learn and accept that there is something beyond that which we know, the more our judgment becomes balanced. Rage and fury become less prevalent once we can accept our place in the universe. If we could look into the souls of people who commit violent acts, we would probably see the very same emotions that are imprisoned inside of us. Those of us who have a slight inkling of a world beyond the known, however, can cope more easily with the vicissitudes of their own narrow experience. Gifted children can broaden our vision and help us deal with the frustration of our limited perspectives.[9]

One way to broaden our perspective is to accept both the good and the bad in our emotional life. Sometimes, the only emotions acceptable to us are the positive ones, and goodness comes to eclipse badness. As a result, children are never taught to cope with their negative feelings. Instead, they suppress them.

At Roeper School, we used to have something called "human relations," and we discussed anything that came up. At Thanksgiving time, I remember a discussion with the children about what it was like to get ready for Thanksgiving and to experience it oneself. The children would initially say how happy they were that their grandparents were coming to dinner and how much they had enjoyed previous Thanksgivings. But as I probed a little more, some other, less positive feelings came out. They felt a pressure about being told, "Be a good boy." The children said things like, "I had to stay outside the house so I wouldn't get the floor dirty because my mother just cleaned it. She was impatient with me because she was so busy. And then the cousins came, and we did have fun, and I especially liked the middle one who was just about my age, but how they messed up my toys! All of a sudden, they weren't my toys anymore; I had to share them. And I didn't feel like kissing my aunt—she had a strange smell about her—and really I was glad when they left. But I felt so guilty! They're my cousins and I'm supposed to love them, even if they do show off a lot and if they're bigger than me and sometimes hit me. They brought me a model airplane set and I was supposed to put it together, and I'll tell you a secret—I never did! And then, I was supposed to send a thank-you note for the model airplane that I never wanted anyway!"

If we create an environment where children can express all feelings, then they will have an easier time negotiating the ultimate complexity of life itself. Instead, we create a pretend world where we act as though the emperor were wearing clothes, and we do this because we think that our limited world is the whole world and we have to make it work. These are some of the consequences of our inability to accept the Self and the fact of the unknown unless we embellish them with moral judgments and other visions coming from our limitations.

If we really were coping with spirituality, with the world beyond our world which is not known to us, then there would be less tension in the way in which we live our daily lives, and we could enjoy a changed perspective. The unknown world, which I've been describing as being outside of us, also exists inside. We don't really understand our feelings; who can explain feelings of love, longing, need for others? And we never deal with the concept of sex, which I believe also, in some way, belongs both in the physical and also the spiritual world, and of course, our strange denial leads to the same dark place as all denial.

The Imaginary Companion Is Real

The imaginary companion makes his whimsical appearance in the most unexpected places. There are few families that have not been home to his presence and where he was received with a chuckle. When he does appear, people will cope with his presence in many different ways, but he is never taken entirely seriously. There are those parents who feel it is their parental duty to point out at every opportunity that he doesn't exist, and we have all seen the crestfallen expressions in the faces and eyes of their children. These children will usually turn away and withdraw even further into their own imaginary world, keeping it a secret from their nay-saying parents. Then there are those families that go along with a child's playfulness with a tongue-in-cheek attitude and indulge the childish soul. And there are those who accept the imaginary companion respectfully as part of the inner growth of the child. It is the child of this last family who will experience life more freely. The reality is that the imaginary companion is a most important, respectable component in the child's growth. This is particularly true for the gifted child.

To understand why gifted children need imaginary companions, it is important to keep in mind that gifted children may be overwhelmed by the overabundance of sensations in the world. These are children who may hear an airplane minutes before anyone else does, children who need dark glasses because the light penetrates more deeply to them than to others, children who get sick to their stomachs when they smell particular odors which others may not even experience, children who can't bear clothing that seems too rough or too constricting. Loaded with all that sensitivity, the highly gifted child experiences a world beyond what the rest of us imagine.[10]

All of this is part of the child's inner life in response to the intensive demands of the outside world. The gifted child feels an overload of experiences, expectations, and the most extreme desire to make emotional sense of it all. The lucky child is the one whose umbilical cord has extended outside the womb, because he or she possesses a safe companion, usually a mother, who can to some extent share this burden of experience. But even the lucky children often feel overwhelmed by their ultimate solitude. They can deal with this by inventing a companion, or a whole family, or even countries complete with a language and sets of laws and even constitutions. This imaginary population is always at their disposal, and it can be enlisted to help these children to change their world to make it safe. Multiple companions may have different roles, such as problem solving or soothing pain.

These companions within the Self endow the Self with a sense of power. There is Eva, who has to live with the stress of shuttling back and forth between the two halves of her divorced family. But inside, in Eva-land, everyone lives together, peacefully; animals never devour each other, and there is great safety. We can see that the imaginary companion is not just a whimsical invention of the little child, but a most important component that makes life bearable. With an imaginary companion, life becomes a shared experience instead of an unrelentingly lonely one.

As we grow older, we find that this imaginary companion remains with us in some form or another all through life and continues to make certain situations bearable. It may also create problems for us, because we may have a tendency to extend fantasies about our imaginary companion to the reality of our daily life and then to try to impose expectations on our mates, our parents, and our children. People who have no love life, for example, invent one and dream of exciting adventures with their perfect mate. But then, when a real person comes along, he or she may have trouble measuring up.

In many ways, our children become the embodiment of our imaginary companion, who in turn is the object of our dream. These imaginary expectations, which can take so many different forms, often affect the daily life of a family to a much greater extent than we realize. This is especially true where gifted children are concerned. They can be expected to fulfill the dreams of their parents, their teachers, or sometimes even whole communities. Though this may seem farfetched, there are imaginary companions not only for individuals, but for whole groups of people. If a group assigns the role of imaginary companion to a child, the attendant expectations may produce guilt and anxiety. There is a story by Hermann Hesse called "Beneath the Wheel" about a child in a rural community who turns out to be a genius. He participates in national competitions, and the community's hopes for fame rest heavily on him. The boy in the story is forced to spend his summer studying and preparing while his age mates are out fishing and swimming. Being the imaginary companion—the perfect child—for this community becomes an overwhelming burden.

In its original, more limited conception, however, the imaginary companion may remain the basic support for the young person facing the vicissitudes of a stressful life. It behooves us to provide a sanctuary for our imaginary companion. May he never feel that he doesn't exist!

Chapter 7

Legitimacy

Many of us feel we are not legitimate in the eyes of those in charge. We've accepted that there is a hierarchy of values and rights. White men have more power than white women in our society today. To be a gay person carries with it a stigma; to be a Jew has often carried the same stigma; to be African-American has always meant carrying a burden of illegitimacy. And in our schools, we find that gifted children don't feel that their needs are legitimate in the eyes of their teachers.

Those who are viewed as illegitimate frequently act out their enormous need to become legitimate by doing the types of things that are accepted by society. We saw this need expressed, for instance, in the rush by gay people who got married when the mayor of San Francisco, Gavin Newsom, opened the door to them. After World War I, German Jews became more and more assimilated into the German culture, and yet they did not feel completely legitimate. They tried to be more German than most Germans. A large number of young Jewish men volunteered for the First World War, and many of them died on the battlefield. Much as they tried, they could not achieve total legitimacy or equality, and they seldom advanced in the military.

One way in which we make ourselves legitimate, in our own eyes and in the eyes of others, is through titles. We also make ourselves legitimate by living through others. When I grew up in Germany as a child, doctors were mostly men—women doctors were very rare. Indeed, my mother was one of the first, but typically women gained legitimacy by hitching on to somebody else. Wives of medical doctors were addressed as "Frau Doktor." But inside, they always knew that the title wasn't quite their own.

We cover ourselves with titles and honors as we cover our bodies with clothes. Being legitimate in the eyes of others can become quite an emotional burden for the Self of a person. "Who am I?" is the eternal question that every human being asks, and we find the answer either by looking into ourselves, or by measuring ourselves against others, or both. There is a tension inside every Self between the drive to fulfill its own, internal agenda and the need to see oneself through the eyes of others. Those eyes, of course, are biased and controlled by a kind of unconscious agreement known as public opinion. Everything gets measured against this undefined (and not officially acknowledged) measurement. It is within the context of this public opinion, which has such authority over our soul, that we try to self-actualize.

In my lifetime, I've seen many strands of emotional growth toward self-actualization. The first one that I actually participated in and experienced with all my heart was the Civil Rights Movement. It was most interesting for this young woman who came from Germany and had experienced racism in its cruelest form to watch it here all over again. Clearly, African-Americans were seen as inferior by whites, and to some extent by themselves. I witnessed the emotional growth and the rise of the Black Self, led by Dr. Martin Luther King, Jr. Our school at that time was one of the first to be racially integrated, and I could see firsthand the individual growth of our Black parents and their children and how their Selves came into their own.

To watch some of these children grow was an emotional experience in itself. There was a beautiful little three-year-old girl, as quick as any child I'd seen. She learned to read in no time, and it was clear that the accepting environment allowed her to be herself. She had to go through a rather strange experience, though, in her own growth, because since we did not have many African-American children and because she was so charming and creative, her vision of herself wasn't checked by her peers and grew somewhat beyond realistic limits. As she grew older (she went to our school for many years), her status as the little princess of the school declined. Because her self-esteem had become dependent on outside admiration, when that disappeared, she experienced some difficult times maintaining her belief in her own Self. We had to help her regain a more realistic acceptance of herself based on her *own* belief in herself.

The Civil Rights Movement spawned the Women's Movement, and again I looked at it through the eyes of an observer. I could see that the developmental phases that a movement went through correlated with the developmental stages of the Self. Each woman had to find her own way of growing into equality with men. It was interesting to watch this gender drama play out with gifted children. There was one brilliant little girl who formed an alliance with her physicist father that absolutely left out the mother, who was seen by both as the subservient housewife. The mother's spirit became increasingly meek as the daughter spread her emotional and intellectual wings, sharing and understanding the father's scientific discoveries. Before the Women's Movement, the child would not have felt the freedom to develop in her own right. This girl actually became a scientist, but the whole situation led to the divorce of the parents.

The Women's Movement had an interesting effect on children, because women needed to be involved with their own emotional growth and their own relationship to themselves. The need for the personal growth of the individual woman influenced her relationships to her children. We noticed at our school that there were times when a woman might put her own growth before that of her children. Mothers might come too late to pick up their children, and children could feel superfluous. This was a time when behavior problems at our school for the gifted were much more pronounced. I remember an incident when one little boy said to another, "It doesn't matter what you say; we're just pollution." It was a period when many children were not at the center of their mother's attention, and not much thought was given to fostering their Self and their creativity.

The gifted, with their strong degree of sensitivity, were even more likely to feel that they had been left to their own devices.

In recent years, I've seen many examples of parents who brought their gifted children to see me for an evaluation, and a strange thing would happen in my interactions with them. As I was discussing their children's life experiences, there would almost invariably be a discussion of the parents' early lives. In many cases, parents would speak of how they did not feel understood by their families and felt lonely, as though they didn't belong (which is just another way of saying they didn't feel legitimate). I've had several parents who broke into tears, and when I asked why, the answer was that they envied their children for being truly accepted into the world.

A generation ago, it was harder to be a gifted child. It was a time when we would look at a gifted child and see his hyperactivity as a sign of pathology. It was just not legitimate to be gifted. We would look at children who didn't fit our narrow definition of what a child should be and find them wanting. Today we might recognize this child as gifted, but in those days, it wasn't legitimate to be different. Loneliness would creep into all of their relationships and dampen their spirits. It was the equivalent to a flower growing in dry sand.

During this time, women came into their own, became secure in their positions, and created their own lifestyles. After a long time, new habits and customs developed, and relationships between the members of the family took many spiraling turns into new approaches to childrearing. As both men and women became more secure in their new positions, they began to look away from themselves and each other and to discover their children. After it became legitimate to be a woman with her own inner agenda, children finally became legitimate. We always knew that there were illegitimate children, but we never realized that there were periods when almost all children were illegitimate in terms of their rights for developing their inner Self. But as so often happens, a new trend was born, unobserved by most—a new movement, which has not yet been named, and I name it the Children's Movement.

The change has occurred subtly. It has been supported by the modern opportunities for mobility and the advent of the computer. In the past, parents might choose to live in different cities for the sake of their own career needs, and children would have to move where their parents moved. Now, parents are more willing to change their own arrangements for the benefit of their child. One person I know shook her head in disbelief when her business partner left their medical group to move to a city with a more appropriate school for his five-year-old daughter. Grandmothers shake their heads and say, "You're spoiling that child rotten." The surprising result, however, is that these children have a great sense of freedom, and there is much less of a power struggle between them and their parents. Where children have become truly legitimate, there is much less rivalry between siblings, because there is less of a need to maintain their position of power in order to protect their Self. If both parents and children feel legitimate in their own right, their creativity can express itself in amazing, unforeseeable ways.

When children feel legitimate, their spirit grows, almost without limits. Juxtapose this with a child who comes from a family background based on strict deference to authority. In the latter family system, you will find a child who feels defeated in her attempt to stretch her emotional limbs. In fact, she takes on the beliefs of the power structure and feels guilty for not being able to make herself do the expected homework, even though her boredom feels limitless. Of course, we never know where the next movement is going to take us, but the early years of this century could be years in which more gifted children are seen as legitimate by their families.

Chapter 8

The New Children and the Unexpected New Perspective

And a woman who held a babe against her bosom said,
Speak to me of Children. And he said:
Your children are not your children.
They are the sons and daughters of life's longing for itself.
They come through you but not from you,
And though they are with you, yet they belong not to you.
You many give them your love but not your thoughts,
For they have their own thoughts.
You may house their bodies but not their souls,
For their souls dwell in the house of tomorrow,
Which you cannot visit, not even in your dreams.
You may strive to be like them, but seek not to make them like you,
For life goes not backward nor tarries with yesterday.
You are the bows from which your children as living arrows
*   are sent forth.*
The Archer sees the make upon the path of the infinite,
And He bends you with His might that His arrows may go
*   swift and far.*
Let your bending in the Archer's hand be for gladness,
For even as He loves the arrow that flies,
So He loves also the bow that is stable.

~Kahlil Gibran[11]

began my consultation service in Oakland in the early 1980s. I had worked for many years with gifted children at the Roeper School, which I founded with my husband George. We had always taken as part of our mission the creation of a community for children and adults that would allow their inner Selves to grow freely in a supportive environment. This, we believed, would lead them to participate in the community of the world. When children are allowed this kind of freedom, they begin to feel a responsibility for the world beyond themselves. Because they are not so preoccupied with having to protect their own Selves, they can look at the world with available emotional strength.

After retiring from the school, I felt the need to continue my work in a different form, so I founded the Roeper Consultation Service, which I have continued for more than 20 years. I never tire of working with gifted children, because I so frequently encounter that expansive spark of passion and awareness in them, and it totally fascinates me. I know that within these children lies a whole complex reservoir of knowledge and feelings that we adults have forgotten. The individual differences in the inner agenda of these children and the unalterable drive they feel to fulfill it never fails to engage me fully. They may have enormous individual differences, but they share an inner necessity to fulfill their own agendas.

Yet some of them feel a great discomfort because the world around us doesn't know how to receive them. I, myself, am driven by a longing for a different worldview than the one that is generally accepted as the "real" view of the world. I had never believed in the possibility that it might ever change, and yet this had always been my hope. Just like the children I saw in my work, I wanted to feel at home on our planet. Children who opened their souls to me often spoke of being "aliens" in our world; their innermost feelings were so often left unvalidated or were actively discouraged. All I could do was to try to let them know that I understood some of their experiences of reality. They rarely failed to be touched that someone understood, and they seemed to shine with a brighter light after such conversations.

But even I was unprepared for the arrival of a new kind of child and the simultaneous evolutionary changes that seem to be taking place. A new crop of children, heralded by a new kind of parent, has descended upon us: so bright, so knowledgeable, so naturally spiritual and intuitive! Their eyes contain the wisdom of the universe.

Slowly, awareness of the changes began to penetrate my consciousness. I first noticed it in my consultation service: there was a change in the type of children, their behavior, and their parents. There were unprecedented numbers of highly gifted children and a shift in the attitude of their parents. What I had been hoping for all of my life seemed to actually be happening! I have now been struggling for a while to put these insights into words so that I could share them with others. I am not alone in my observations. Others have observed the same phenomenon and found different ways to integrate them into their philosophy. Some German educators in Waldorf schools call them "star children."

I had long been aware of a distinct pattern of expectations coming from each of the three participants involved in the process of growth and education of the child—the parents, the child, and the school. Parents were focused on achievement at school. "How can I make him do his homework? How can I make her fit the expectations of the school? How can I make them be successful and cooperate with the school?" they would ask. They felt that their duty was mainly to help their child succeed in this competitive environment.

Certain behaviors and reactions on the part of the children also repeated themselves regularly. They resisted doing their homework; they felt guilty if they disappointed their parents. They felt that their abilities in art and music were less important than their academic ones. They often felt worthless when they didn't live up to usual expectations. They didn't realize that their achievements in other areas were no less valuable.

The third partner, the school, represented the so-called "real world," which had a clear and common goal for all children. The schools had their own distinct worldview, based on a hierarchical valuation of human beings and on the success model, as opposed to the growth model. Only that which could be proven was seen as real, and only those who surpassed others in their achievement were seen as legitimate. Everyone seemed to accept that these goals were necessary and immutable reality. It was the first duty of parents and schools to set the child on her way down this demanding path so that she could adjust to these expectations.

This led to the parents' strangely contradictory task: they knew that each child was different, and they knew about gifted children being different, but the "real world" needed to be catered to! It was the highest duty of each parent to make children adjust to society's expectations. It was generally accepted that if the adults or the child failed in that endeavor, the consequences would be disastrous. Children experienced love and acceptance as conditional, predicated on their success at fulfilling the demands of the "real world."

Difficulties and conflicts frequently arose, because the agendas of schools diverged from the inner agenda of the child. Most adults were so locked into their concept of the real world that they could not conceive of the child experiencing a different reality. The child, on the other hand, had absolutely no choice but to follow the beat of her own drummer. When this drummer happened to coincide with the demands of the school, the child was lucky, for she felt loved and supported. In this case, the expectations of the adults did not contradict the child's strong inner desires.

Often, however, gifted children (and adults as well) are driven by an inner agenda that diverges from mainstream expectations. Parents and schools often ended up on one side and the child on the other. Schools established the standards, and if a child did not adjust, there were dire consequences. This situation was clearly David against Goliath and created a strain between parents and children. Competition, testing, and grades drove the system. The more highly gifted the children were, the less able they were to succeed in this system, because their way of learning and being, their sense of fairness and justice, and their abhorrence of regimentation meant that their needs did not coincide with those of the system.

The irony was that no matter how highly gifted these children were, they were not accepted into private schools—even, sometimes, special schools for the gifted—and in public schools, they usually got into trouble. One would expect the opposite to be the case—that schools would compete for the gifted—but this was not the case, because society did not understand the gifted in its midst and felt threatened by their passionate drives and abilities.

Moreover, society's ability to accept the concept of giftedness was limited by the societal concept of normality. The result was that children were under enormous pressure to conform. Many parents sided with the system. There were fights, discussions, and depressions for both parents and children. Competition between siblings was fierce. Parents reported a great deal of tension and found it difficult to raise gifted children. There were also heroes, namely those children who could successfully negotiate the tensions they lived under without surrendering their essential sense of Self. Slowly, parents became aware of the pressure on their children, and many began to home school them.

The most highly gifted often became the outcasts of society. For example, a highly gifted man who wished for his children to receive an education paid for it by driving a laundry truck most of his life. I knew a highly gifted woman who had a job working with children. She was loved by them, but because she had never been able to obtain a degree, she earned so little money that she could not manage. She left the work and chose instead at a menial job that paid her more money. Many highly gifted people, either because they are not interested or because they are not able to move beyond the fringe of society, live on the edge of poverty. There are many artists, musicians, and other creative people whose outstanding potential is of little use to themselves or to others. On the other hand, there are wonderful jobs for the mainstream gifted who have performed well within the expected framework. There are many who are highly gifted but lead lives outside the mainstream without financial or personal stability, status, or recognition. They have found themselves in a kind of oblivion. Their needs remain largely unfulfilled and their talents unused.

There are also some who voluntarily opt out of the mainstream activities. One highly gifted man, a partner in a well-known law firm, left his career to stay home and do research and scientific experiments based on the Bible. He never published his findings, and his talents were lost to society. I once had a most interesting correspondence with a young man imprisoned for stealing. He was very good at it but was finally caught. Finding me on the Internet was, according to him, a lifesaver. In his letters to me, he wondered how different things might have been had his all-encompassing love and talent for music not been ridiculed by his father in childhood.

Many gifted children had, and still do have, a most difficult time all during their school careers because they simply did not fit in. These difficulties are expressed in many different ways, such as an inability to concentrate on homework or sit still in boring classes. Demetrius, for instance, could simply never face any work at school, but he was so brilliant and had so much loving support that he finally graduated from high school after almost flunking out. Beginning at age nine, he was doing activist work and gave inspiring speeches based on his overwhelming desire to save the world. Among other things, he was trying to help the homeless.

Albert Einstein attended school sporadically, but ultimately, he felt that a lack of schooling was the best thing that happened to him. It allowed him to be free to pursue his own inner agenda. I have known many other children who have made similar choices.

Until about the end of the 20th Century, there were not many children who were recognized as extremely highly gifted, and those who were had little support from society. They were different and therefore suspect. Many new labels were attached to these children: Attention Deficit Disorder (ADD) and other learning disabilities; also autism and other psychological disorders. Children were brought to my consultation service with a list of labels. A typical parent's lament began: "I believe that my child is gifted, but the psychologist says he needs to be on Ritalin®. He is so overexcitable. He does not sit still in class. Yet he can concentrate on the computer, listen to music, write wonderful poetry, and play soccer. His handwriting is terrible." "All of these characteristics are signs of giftedness," I would reply.

I deeply believe that there is a huge misunderstanding of the soul—not only the soul of gifted children, but of all children and ultimately our own souls as well. Our standards are so rigid that we call some of these children "twice-exceptional"—gifted and ADD, for example. Giftedness is, in many cases, confused with pathology. We have, for instance, known for a long time that overexcitability (OE), a concept developed by Kazimierz Dabrowski,[12] is one of the characteristics of giftedness, yet we don't accept its expression as a normal characteristic of the gifted. OE is often difficult to handle, so we simply put a negative label on the child instead of trying to create appropriate structures, such as an open classroom which does not require as many hours sitting at a desk.

I remember a six-year-old boy who simply could not sit in a chair and was always running around the classroom. The teachers thought he was not learning and were immensely surprised to find out that he was actually reading at a third-grade level.

Passionate reaction to inner and outer stimuli is a "symptom" of giftedness that can often express itself in OE. The most extreme acting out often comes from the child who can't live up to the enormously high expectations he places on himself. I know a six-year-old boy who studies hamsters and their heredity and raises different strains of these animals. When his experiments don't work out, he has a screaming temper tantrum.

In my consultations, I often find myself confronted by parents who are confused by their children's so-called behavior problems. It always comes as a great relief when I can convince them of two things: first, that the child needs them on their side; and second, that the problem isn't their child's "disability," but rather the conflict between the passion of the child and the rigid expectations of the school.[13]

When parents are able to change their attitudes, the child almost invariably changes some of his behavior, even if the school remains unchanged. Theo was always in trouble at school, interrupting, not getting his homework done, and distracting others. He went from school to school. Everybody in his environment saw only the problems he created, not the brilliant, sensitive person he was. In my conversation with him, I was amazed at his adult way of expressing himself and his self-knowledge. Mostly, though, I was touched by his agony. What he needed was simple but important. "I would like that just once things will go my way," he told me with tears in his eyes. He needed some recognition and power for his inner Self. In my conversation with his mother, I told her that Theo needed her to recognize his inner Self as distinct from her. This prompted his mother to call one morning with the following question: "Theo does not want to go to school today. He is not sick. Would it be a good idea if I let him stay home?" I told her that I thought it would be a very good idea to try it just this once. She did, and there was a small but immediate change in the child's behavior. After a number of sessions with me, a real change in attitude occurred in parent and child. The teachers were surprised, and the tension eased a great deal.

These were the types of situations I often dealt with in my practice. I suffered with these children. I felt unable to help them in any significant way. More and more, I realized that I had been one of them in my time and that by trying to help them, I was also trying to help myself. Giftedness was not the real problem. The problem was that we were living in two different worlds and had no real way of connecting! I did not expect that it would ever change. I tried to ease the situation by focusing attention on the Self of the child, as well as on the dilemma in which loving parents found themselves. I was often able to help individual children and adults simply by showing them a different point of view.

Two exciting developments all of a sudden reached my consciousness and changed my thinking: namely, the emergence of the new children, and the changing attitudes of parents. These two events have far-reaching consequences, which for me, though unobserved by most people, have been unexpected miracles. It seems as though an oppressive darkness has been lifted from my soul and turned into an infinite sky, complete with sparkling stars.

It was around the millennium that I became aware of different topics and concerns of parents seeking my advice. From that point on, a great transformation has seemed to gain momentum. Looking back, two dramatic changes appeared simultaneously in my consultation work, and they soon merged to become one. First, more and more parents were beginning to speak about their children in a different manner. They showed new attitudes about their children and raised new concerns. They talked more about their children's feelings, creativity, and special characteristics and less about adjustments and behavior problems. At the same time, there was a clearly noticeable increase in giftedness. While in the past, most gifted children's IQ scores were around 140 or 150, now 175 to 200 have become frequent occurrences. All of the typical characteristics of the highly gifted—enormous sensitivity, spirituality, a desire to change the world, and intensity—also markedly increased. It is as though parents now realize that they need to do more than just prepare the child for the competitive world. They need to create an environment in which the child's Self can flourish, rather than just adjust to the demands of the system.

Now I see a growing number of parents who are passionately committed to creating the appropriate niche for their child in the world in general, and in the world of education specifically. I can see this change not only in the way parents deal with their children, but also in the way that they engage the learning environment. Instead of attending parent-teacher conferences with the expectation of finding out how their child is performing, they have begun to turn the tables and tell teachers about their child's emotional characteristics and needs. In the past, parents and schools both tried to make the child live up to the school's expectations; now parents search for the school environment that will best accommodate their child, including home schooling. This means that the constellation has changed—no longer is it the case that school and parents gang up against child; instead, parent and child are on the same side with the school.

This new constellation has resulted in the increase in both the number of gifted children and their levels of giftedness. It was as though we had been blocking the light from a fertile piece of ground. The seeds had always been there, but the goals and attitudes of society stunted their growth. Once we stepped aside, they began to germinate and grow to their fullest heights.

Marc is an excellent math student. He's eight years old, and he can solve mathematical problems that are typically beyond the understanding of children his age. In his mathematical thinking, he is clearly three or four years ahead of his classmates. He astounds his teachers by solving difficult problems involving geometry. The problem comes when his teachers want him to tell them how he arrived at the answers to these problems. He is often not able to, and this has led to great conflict, first between the child and his teacher, and later between the whole family and the school. In the end, Marc had to leave the school. His outstanding gift became a liability for him. He tried very hard to fulfill the requirements of the school but did not succeed.

I don't believe that we can explain this phenomenon any more than we can explain how a self-taught reader learns to read. It must be a specific kind of intuitive growth or ability. The cruel irony is that this talent can hurt the child when he has to defend himself against the demand that he explain himself. The demand to prove everything is based on a kind of distrust. A child's knowledge is actually his or her private possession.[14]

Orion was the first of the new wave of highly gifted and self-aware children. Until he came along, I thought that I had seen and known the whole range of gifted children. In his mother's words, this seven-year-old boy is an "old soul" with an enormous sensitivity toward his own past. He is one of those rare children who appears to have a memory of the moments right after birth. He actually remembers the womb as pink and warm. He functions well only when enveloped by his parents' love. He is deeply, emotionally connected to both parents. His mother surrounds him with a necessary inner coverlet of security. His relationship with her indicates that in some way, he has not severed the emotional umbilical cord. This makes it possible for him to experience life as freely as he wishes.

While his emotional sensitivity renders him vulnerable, it also allows him to be close to his peers and other living things. He feels empathy toward everything around him, whether people, animals, trees, or even stones. He has a special affinity for trees; he cries and feels hurt when he sees them being cut down. He feels their injury. He also feels that rocks are alive; he assured me that they speak to him.

It is hard to imagine the richness of life experience that dwells inside a child like Orion. If he is ever involved in hurting anyone, he is overcome with tremendous guilt. If this happens, he might tell his mother to slap him or punish him in some other way. He will lose a game on purpose when he realizes that if he wins, the other child might be hurt by losing.

Orion is one of a new generation of children who seem to be the avant-garde of the evolution of the human species. He is most sensitive to every event that touches him. For him, every experience is deep and personal. Watching him reminded me of listening to a finely tuned instrument. He does not fit into any of our present categories. He is driven by his inner agenda that leads him to function in areas outside the accustomed boundaries.

Children like Orion, supported by loving parents, are beginning to change the power structure in traditional education. This can threaten some in the educational community. Previously, parents catered to the demands of the school; now, they are beginning to make their own demands in support of their children. Thankfully, more and more parents are supporting their children's inner agendas, and their newfound support seems to be creating a new pattern of growth for children. New customs of family life are developing—for instance, while in the past it was deemed necessary for young children to learn to sleep by themselves and sharing the bed with parents was taboo, now there are families who find it preferable. By accepting the child's Self as the priority, parents have opened the door to the reality of the child's inner agenda. It's as though the child's Self has felt a breath of fresh air, lifted its emotion head, and grown bigger than before because the parental stricture had been removed. I believe that the Selves of these children are free to stretch their emotional limbs and begin to grow. Just as physically we grow taller today than we did 100 years ago, so our emotions are expanding in many directions.

When parental attitudes undergo such a fundamental trans-formation, the children themselves take on new characteristics. They are each unique and yet have much in common. They appear to be born with a different, more expanded concept of reality. Their reality transcends the visible and provable to include things we don't see and can't prove. These children feel the mystery and the beauty and the strangeness in the world. The newborn has feelings before she has words. Nothing is more real than anything else; hunger for food, hunger for love—all are equal in her world. Because many parents are accommodating this new understanding, their children are able to continue to live in their expanded reality. These are the children who explain how they feel the soul in trees and remember the pink of the womb. I grew up in the "age of reason," but I also learned how to experience without preconceived judgment, and I believe these children.

The following is a conversation that I had with a highly gifted young child whose knowledge of scientific concepts was astounding. I told him that he confused me because it seemed like he was always mixing magic with science. "But that is the same thing," he replied. He was struggling with the concept of the unknown. He may not have had it quite sorted out, but just as he has to learn from us, we also have to learn from him as well. We need to include the unknown in our understanding of reality. These children continue to include the magical and the unknown in their thoughts and feel-ings because they have not been forced to suppress this knowledge.

Freed from the crippling constraints and inner struggles of previous generations, the new children are driven by an enormous life force. They find their real world so exciting that they can hardly contain themselves. Seeing these children, we can truly appreciate how hard it has been in the past for children forced to suppress their driving life force. They felt guilty for being driven by their inner excitement and agenda. They did not know how to contain it, and this led to struggles. It was like a river was flowing wildly and happily on its way, when we dammed it for our own purposes and made it into a placid, beautiful, useful little lake. Imagine the quantity of energy that went into the containment of the life force. Now we have released this awesome volume of energy. Paradoxically, we contain this energy for fear of what will happen if it is allowed to run free, yet it is only a frightening force when contained. Free and left to flow where it will, it is a force of joy and life.

I see child after child who is now free to pursue her destiny. These children's holistic point of view often blurs the line between themselves and others, because their highly developed empathy drives them to sense the feelings of others. There is the 10-year-old who wants to help younger children who have emotional problems. There is the 14-year-old who says, "We must change the world, and we young people will!" There is the six-year-old who collects pennies from her classmates for the children of Iraq so that "they will have something to cuddle at night." And there is the 15-year-old cellist who is totally committed to becoming a globally known performer in order to share her love of music with others. Examples like these show what children can do when they are allowed to follow their passion and when their efforts are supported by adults.

One of the other differences I see is the great variety of children's talents and abilities in the cognitive, emotional, artistic, and athletic areas. Most gifted children combine several of them. Many have a love and need for music; many are athletes or performers; others are budding architects with their Lego® sets. The most amazing thing to me is the way that these children are bringing their creativity to conventional fields such as medicine, mathematics, and computer science. They may love Shakespeare and Mozart, but they also love gardening and much else. Children with so much talent and passion across so many disciplines show me the power of their newly discovered freedom.

Chapter 9

Self-Actualization
and Interdependence

The most outstanding feature of our reality is the total inter-dependence of all things on earth—animate and inanimate. Though we cannot escape the reality of this fact, our thoughts and emotions cannot truly grasp it. For too long, we have divided the world between opposing concepts—between the dependency of the many and the independence of a few, between the powerful and the powerless. Furthermore, we have disrupted the ecology of our planet and exploited nature, believing we are its masters. Our manner of appropriating and wasting resources is tearing apart the very fabric that sustains life on this planet.

We have failed to understand that all living things are defined by what they feel themselves to be and not by what they do. We are motivated to fulfill the needs of the "I" of our innermost being. This drive is conscious and unconscious motivation for all of our actions. Only when we achieve inner satisfaction can we truly understand the miracle of interdependence, for it is also the miracle of our intercon-nectedness to each other. We know that gifted children experience the world through their expanded senses: they hear distant sounds long before others do; they suffer from music that is too loud; they experi-ence sights, odors, touch, and taste beyond the usual limits of our senses. Global awareness among gifted individuals is more than geo-graphical or political; it is an emotional and spiritual acceptance of the unknown. Yet the gifted are most fascinated by the here and now. They may feel the life in every tree and flower. Animals may be their truest friends; they truly communicate with them, and the relationships they form can penetrate their body and soul. The smallest detail in nature excites them, and they can create a symphony by hitting two sticks against each other. Nature, music, art, people—anything they experience on this earth—evoke strong emotional reactions in them.

The global awareness of gifted children includes awareness of the universe, as well as awareness of every detail in daily life. This awareness inspires their creativity. It is the task of the adult to open the door to all of these experiences and activities to the soul of the gifted child—and keep it open. This is accomplished by the adult's emotional acceptance of the child's Self. Once we accept the expanded reality in which these children are living, we cannot help but change our own perceptions and actions, including a different approach to the purpose and process of education.

It is clear to many adults that there is a vast gap between that which drives gifted children—their curiosity and desire—and the established goals of education. This gap between the way children grow and the way we teach them causes a great many difficulties and apparent failures. These are often interpreted as disabilities or problems within the child, while the reality is that the methods and goals of education do not really meet the needs of the child and his or her goals. We need to take a critical look at the goals of education and the methods and systems that we have built to further these goals. Through my many years of involvement in gifted education, I have developed an alternative structure and set of goals for education, which I call Self-Actualization and Interdependence.

Self-Actualization and Interdependence (SAI) is a concept encompassing the goals, the process, and the content of education. It differs in many fundamental ways from the traditional model. It is not a variation or radical swing of the pendulum. It is based on an entirely different philosophy of life that stems from a different view of the individual, the world, and the universe. How does SAI view the individual and the world? It looks at both from the inside out and from the "I" of the beholder.[15]

Every action is, in the end, motivated by our inner agenda and the way that our life appears to us. The study of the Self in general and the individual in particular is essential to the SAI approach, for it has many characteristics that we are not aware of. Essential to the SAI approach is the fact that the Self always sees alternatives. It determines its own imperatives and may choose an alternative which, from the cultural or societal point of view, may seem unreasonable. It may need to evade outside control, but in so doing, it may create an obstacle and have to choose another alternative. For example, a 15-year-old boy was deeply involved in writing a novel. Seeing his schoolwork slip, his parents were worried that he wouldn't graduate. He evaded outside control by locking himself up in his room. From the parents' and the school's point of view, his behavior was unreasonable and unrealistic, but the boy was driven by his Self's need to write, which superseded those expectations. To follow the passion of his Self, he chose to neglect his schoolwork. For him, this was the only alternative to denying the inner imperative of his Self.

The essential goal of SAI is to understand the Self as an autonomous decision-maker. The survival and growth of the Self, as well as the connection to other Selves, is the individual's highest priority. This is the true meaning of interdependence. Self-actualization means that the goal of the Self may differ from that of society. In the SAI concept, we place the needs of the Self before the needs of society. The "I," this complex inner universe, cannot be denied and is a concept that needs to be considered in our perception of the individual and, indeed, in all human endeavor.[16]

Moreover, the Self needs connection to other Selves. So while it grows, it builds bridges to the outside. It is the task of adults to facilitate bridge-building. The growing Self needs the lifeline of connection, first to the parents and then to others. To create loving, supportive relationships is the first task of the adult. Within this lifeline of the relationship, growth and learning in many different areas take place. All Selves need to be rooted in supportive relationships.

These may include living things in nature, as well as inanimate objects.

The Self contains a multitude of hidden emotions—passions of love, desire, and creativity. As it begins its journey of growth, it needs the support of other Selves and society as a whole. When this support does not exist, the Self may not grow in the preordained manner and may turn these feelings into their opposite, such as hate and anxiety. Our world is frequently turned into a battlefield for conflicted Selves, while well-supported Selves are eager to participate in the world and transform it in constructive ways.

It follows that SAI offers a different view of community and human interaction. SAI sees the earth and the universe as a total network of interdependence. SAI is open to the fact that every event or action may have multiple unexpected results. Just as one event or action may spill over into another, the Self has an intricate web of relationships and is not entirely self-contained. Instead, it flows into connection with the surrounding community, as well as with the mysterious unknown around us which we call the universe.

The SAI Philosophy and Education

The SAI philosophy can lead to a redefinition of every aspect of education. It begins with the recognition of the uniqueness of each individual, his or her enormous inner complexity, hidden resources and drives, and inner goals and characteristics. This recognition, by itself, can change attitudes and approaches toward parenting and redefine the goals, processes, structures, and content of education. SAI includes the awareness of the limits of language and logic. It requires trusting one's intuition, empathizing, and understanding that there are many ways to communicate which are unspoken and nonverbal. SAI is aware of the complex, often unconscious inter-action between different Selves, such as children, parents, teachers, and peer groups, and it recognizes the importance of unconscious and spiritual growth.

Out of the SAI concept develops a different model of education. It is a growth-based model, not a success-based one. In the growth-based model, the Self is seen as healthy, not pathological. The Self wants to grow and learn, not to be fixed. SAI sees the tasks of learning and teaching from a different perspective. SAI sees a child's inner agenda as part of reality, and it defines that reality in a manner consistent with the child's perspectives, which may be different from those of adults.

A growth-based model starts from the inside and works its way out. It understands the complexity of the Self and its own curriculum for growth. It understands that the Self not only guards itself with many defense mechanisms, but it also contains many different hidden sources of energy, such as empathy, altruism, creativity, and love. The Self is driven by a basic life force. Its emotional and intellectual reactions depend on both its outer and inner experiences. All actions take place against the background of the Self's life experiences. The unknown, inner world of the Self may account for a child's acting out or her failure to conform to expectations.

The role of academics changes within the SAI context. It becomes imbedded in the growth model, not separate or superior as in the success model. The young Self is driven to take up his proper place and exert his impact on the world. Thus, the Self is not just a receptacle for information about the world, but is an actor in it. Growth springs from emotion, but it needs our intellectual powers to understand.

The growth of the Self within the supportive community is a goal of education in SAI. Success and competition are not excluded in the growth model, but they are not seen as defining the individual's value. For example, the love connection between parent and child must be unconditional, independent of a child's success. This, however, is a complex, often unconscious process, because the Self of teachers or parents is enmeshed in the history of success of the child.

We can strive toward finding ways of helping the child by trying to understand our own emotional heritage. This sort of self-exploration is one way to learn more about the intricate life of the Self. Therefore, in the SAI model, teachers and parents must look at their own conscious and unconscious emotions as they affect their relationships with the child, honoring both the child's needs and their own. It is essential to establish honest accommodations for each other and to focus as much on relationships as on other areas.

Traditional education is based mostly on the apparent needs of society. It often ignores the existence of the Self and its power to resist external control. It does not ask the question of the validity of the inner agenda or its hidden capacities or resources, nor does it question the validity of its own expectations. According to this point of view, education starts from the outside in. Traditional education expects the Self to cooperate with its demands, regardless of whether the Self is able and willing to comply. This is especially distressing to the Self, which is trapped in a system of someone else's priorities and values that may not be trusted by the Self.

Any philosophy of education is only as good as its implementation. The traditional approach has developed and changed throughout history. At this point in history, we see society as the vague entity which tries to protect the individuals within the group. Society establishes laws, rules, and goals, all of which are meant to build and protect the community and thereby benefit the individual within it. The process of education is the vehicle through which we try to integrate the growing individual into the ranks of society, and over time, certain concepts and approaches become accepted. The values of the dominant society are seen as the ones traditional education strives to meet.

The traditional approach defines human beings in terms of what they can do and how they can serve, not in terms of who they are. Cows serve by giving milk, but how they feel about their donation is never considered. Society has decided which expectations are nonnegotiable. As cows are expected to give milk, so human beings are expected to develop their physical skills and thinking skills, but in prioritizing these values, we have ignored the enormous power of the Self and the complex inner life of each individual.

Society does not see the world as interdependent, but rather as divided between those at the top of the hierarchy and those who serve them. This traditional model, which causes fierce competition, is based on power, and education is enlisted in the cause of furthering the interests of the powerful. The child is seen as a tool to serve society, and children are taught to see themselves as striving to be the best tool they can be so that they can develop skills to win by gaining power and fame.

Over the centuries, we have seen that this framework does not work. It has led to the belief that humankind is the master of the world, which it is not. Moreover, it has led to great destruction and tragedy for the earth and humankind.

Comparison Table: SAI Model vs. Traditional Model

SAI/Growth Model	Traditional/Success Model
Who am I?	What can I do?
Self-evolvement	Fulfillment of expectations
Growth	Success
Learning	Teaching
Free will	Imposed limitations
Power of Self	Power of society
Never bored	Bored
Inner agenda	Empty vessel
Active learner	Passive learner
Interdependence	Hierarchies
Mutuality	Survival of the fittest
Plurality of causes and effects	Linear cause and effect
Self as power	Self ignored, unknown
Education from inside out	Education from outside in
Relationships	Strategies
Inclusion of the unknown and the mysterious	Conquest of life, making the unknown known
Long-range view	Short-range view
Circle of interdependence; no winners or losers	Belief in winning; winners and losers
Support of ecology	Ignorance of ecology; exploitation

Applying the SAI Model

What kind of environment would accommodate this model? Most of the cultures we now live in have created a hierarchical world. What needs to happen to integrate these concepts into the way people think and feel? How can we make them integral to our way of life? What needs to happen to apply them in practical ways? We can make inroads into the existing structure by remembering the twin concepts of the Self and the interdependence of all of life. With these in mind, we can take aim at new goals for childrearing and education and, in doing so, redefine the task of growing up.

The process begins when a newborn looks with wonder at the world. She must not be expected to submit to the needs of society; instead, she must be allowed to begin the journey of self-discovery and growing a strong Self. This, in turn, will allow her to create a meaningful place for her Self in the world. The task for the child, then, is not a task of simply adjusting to the world, but of living out a goal of Self-actualization. The tiny Self cannot accomplish this alone. She needs the lifeline to the caregiver, a connection that is the metaphorical continuation of the umbilical cord.

In the past, parents have felt the need to consult me when they detected a discrepancy between their child's inner agenda and the expectations of school. In fact, many children—previously well-adjusted children—began struggling when their inner agenda butted up against the school's values. In the tug-of-war between the child and teachers, the parents sought my help in finding ways for the child to fit the school's expectations. None of this need happen in the SAI model.

In the SAI model of education, the parents see their task as helping their child fulfill his own destiny. Parents open the door for the child rather than molding the child into a preconceived shape. To do this, the parents must regard the child as an autonomous, self-contained entity, responsible for its own destiny. This allows the child's inner agenda to drive his learning. The child initiates his own growth and learns the basic skills such as walking and talking without formal teaching. He is in charge of his own mastery. The adults support and guide the unfolding of this destiny, but they cannot create it.

Given what we know about this natural way in which children learn, it is the parents' role to create a safe haven, thus allowing and guiding the unfolding of the child's inner agenda. The unconditional love of the parents acts as a protective cocoon for the growth of the Self. Parents must realize that their acceptance and love is the mainspring for the child's Self-actualization. Children who receive their parents' love and support feel the strength of their Self and the freedom to face the world. Even those who have experienced much trauma, such as physical disability and illness, often exhibit enormous strength and confidence in the world. These are the lucky children; they sparkle with curiosity and passion. The unlucky ones have well-intentioned parents who see society's demands as immutable and leave their children standing alone like David facing Goliath. A shadow invades the Self, even though life seems carefree and protected.

The next development for the growing Self is the integration into community. It is at this point where the difference between traditional education and SAI becomes more apparent. In traditional education, the step into school is often a leap into the realm of numerous expectations. This leap creates a difficult challenge for the Self as it encounters the demands of the outside world head on. The SAI model replaces this artificial leap with organic growth. It is based on a relationship of empathy between child, school, and parents. When a child encounters a world away from home, a world that has a different structure and different expectations, it is important to minimize possible tensions. When the teacher has the mother's trust, the child can have faith that the mother's care will now also flow from the teacher. Through this process, the Self is able to grow and change while remaining fundamentally true to its essence.

The role of the teacher becomes that of a facilitator and observer. At times, the adult may protect the child from emotional and physical injury. But in general, the individual child and the teacher form a more collaborative bond at this point, for together they are wandering into the unknown future of the child.

Traditionally, the teacher has served society as one whose task is to successfully mold children. The teacher's role is pivotal in negotiating the needs of the child and the demands of the school. The adjustment for the child's Self is enormous. Under optimal conditions, the child feels that school is a welcomed adventure and a nurturing, safe environment. Unfortunately, that does not always happen. The difficulties that arise can lead to irreparable damage for the child's Self. Maria Montessori observed:[17]

> *If, during the delicate period of growth, disrespectful demands are inflicted upon the child, his spirit will be diminished and it may never be possible for him to accomplish great deeds as an adult. For such a child must perform the cruel task of hiding his real self, fragmenting it and burying in his subconscious his wealth of aspirations that will forever be unrealized.*

How can the teacher avoid conflict between the powerful world of education and the equally powerful world of the Self of the child? The solution begins with the recognition of the fact that the child's Self is not necessarily bound by the expectations of the educational system. It is the teacher's job to affirm the child's own inner agenda and allow the child to feel that her interests are first and foremost in the classroom.

The teacher must also recognize that children are not empty vessels to be filled with information and rules. Rather, they are individual Selves, each with its own inner agenda. This will require that teachers switch their allegiance from the expectations of society to the growth of the Self. Their mission must change from education for the sake of institutionally measured success to education for sake of Self-actualizing growth. There can be no compromise between meeting the needs of the Self and the needs of society without the Self bearing the cruel burden. While the behavior of the wounded Self can be suppressed, controlled, and squeezed into submission, the fear, anger, hurt, and trauma can have long-term consequences. The SAI model offers a simple solution: the needs of the Self would have priority in the teacher's consideration. In reality, this choice does not even exist, because the Self cannot be totally subjugated, and it will find ways to sabotage expectations. The needs of the Self must always be considered in the interactions and relationships with the child.

There must be an emotional pact between teacher and student, just as has been described before in the primary relationship between child and parent. Children must feel both safe and recognized for who they are as they endeavor to be true to themselves. Teachers, therefore, need to think in terms of relationships rather than strategies. They need to acknowledge that their own Self is an important factor in this relationship and look at their own motivations. Unexpected doors—creatively and academically—will open when children feel that they are in a caring relationship with their teacher.

Teachers must learn to rely on their intuition and empathy in understanding children instead of always relying on the advice of experts. They must realize that there is rarely a precedent for their particular situation, because each relationship is unique. Their goal should be to change the focus from a teacher-centered to a child-centered learning process. SAI redefines curriculum as creating an appropriate environment for emotional and intellectual growth. This curriculum is designed to create a proper place for the Self, where it can grow unhindered in community with other Selves. Original learning and growth take place through relationships based on trust. This trust allows the Self to be open to learn information and skills and to incorporate this knowledge into the world. When a child is driven by the desire to master skills and to make sense of the world, learning can become an adventure filled with excitement, but only if both teacher and student have relatively uncluttered Selves so the growth isn't hindered by anxiety, anger, or ambition.

Learning is an active process. We cannot force a child to learn any more than we can force someone to eat. Children need help in integrating the inner and outer world. There needs to be as much emphasis on expressing their inner world, in whatever form it may take, as there is on learning information about the world around them. The world is filled with exciting things to learn, as well as with many other Selves with whom to interact. In the SAI model, teaching is redefined as facilitating learning rather than imposing knowledge. The content of curriculum and how it is delivered must be constructed on the principles of SAI, and there are many alternative methods of child-centered instruction that can be used within the SAI model.

The role of the group is important in the SAI model. It evolves a life of its own, almost like a separate entity that consists of more than the sum of its members. The attitude, role, and care of the adult are very important in the organic process of group growth. Groups can appear like another being to the observant Self. They can be overwhelming in their power and impact on the Self who wants to join them.

Most traditional classroom groups are controlled by the teacher. This alters the dynamic between and within the individual Selves. In SAI groups of children, the adults don't control the dynamic; rather, they sense the dynamics and are ready to offer an intuitive helping hand whenever it is needed. In the SAI model, this becomes a major task for the teacher.

There is in the growing Self an inherent need for resonance in a community. This community may be school, church, gang, or something else. The natural inborn need for the Self to join with other Selves drives it to affiliate with any community. The nature or purpose of the specific community to which the growing Self becomes attached makes an enormous impact on the growing Self.

The traditional model of education is based on the concept of hierarchy or the notion of survival of the fittest. It is against this background that group members interact. The infrastructure of such a school community consists of many different roles: leaders, followers, protesters, riders on coattails, strengtheners of opposition, jugglers for position, and victims. There are also common dynamics like bonding between these members, protection by leaders, the team concept, and cooperation for the common goal. All of this happens within the hierarchy. It leads to fierce competition and, ultimately, conflict. It creates a vicious dog-eat-dog cycle. The priority of the institution is to satisfy the needs of the top of the hierarchy, not the needs of the individual. In this hierarchical structure, the child is at the bottom, below the teacher, the principal, and so on. This low position leads to the starvation of the child's Self.

The SAI approach departs from this hierarchical worldview. It sees the school as an interactive, living organism that functions like a world in miniature. School encompasses the same human patterns of reactions as the bigger world in which we live, but the SAI school is based on the concept of interdependence rather than hierarchy. It offers the opportunity to develop new approaches that look at the world's achievements and resources as being interconnected and interdependent with all life on earth. Within its worldview, the SAI school incorporates the mysteries of life and death, the unknown within us, and the unknown without. It regards the school community as the place for learning to create mutual support. It prioritizes our intuitive connections with others. It teaches skills of interdependence while understanding the different role of each member of the community. The basic principle of an SAI school is serving the needs of all members of the community, including teachers and support staff, as well as children. This definition of community is especially important to gifted children due to their level of awareness and drive, which amplifies such specific characteristics as their sense of isolation, sense of justice, and the fact that they are global and universal thinkers.

The SAI approaches the school community as a world in miniature. This necessitates a different infrastructure that centers on the growth process. The SAI school becomes a globally interdependent community of learners. A school community offers the opportunity to develop the necessary skills for interdependence. The goals of such a cooperative education community include:

1. To protect the equal rights of each member.

2. To create opportunities to develop skills, attitudes, and the emotional acceptance of the concepts of cooperation and interdependence.

3. To provide learners with an environment that will help them attain their goals.

4. To allow the unhindered growth of Selves whose impact on the world will not have to be distorted, dominated, restricted, or counteracted by their unfulfilled emotional and personal needs.

5. To develop the curriculum of the Self and devise an academic curriculum that will support SAI.

6. To develop in all its members a global vision, which means to see the whole of the community and its ramifications in the world.

7. To develop an understanding of one's rights and obligations in the interdependent community.

8. To see the community as a circle of interdependence, rather than a hierarchy of dependency, with peers and community members as cooperators.

9. To see oneself as a member of the community in four important ways:
   a. to have a stake.
   b. to have a voice.
   c. to have responsibility.
   d. to fulfill a specific task.

10. To see oneself as a valuable and valued member of the community.

I'm offering these principles as an enticement to take a new look at our educational institutions. In order to implement SAI, we will need to redesign our goals, our structures, our attitudes, and the education of teachers and parents. I see this as planting a seed, which now needs to grow through the dedication of the community of learners. The implementation of these principles could have far-reaching ramifications beyond the realm of education.

Chapter 10

Qualitative Assessment:
An Alternative to the IQ Test

When, in 1941, my husband George and I founded Roeper City and Country School in Bloomfield Hills, Michigan, we became aware of the emotional characteristics and educational needs of gifted children. Under the leadership of Dr. Harry Passow, we convened a weeklong, intensive conference of experts to plan a learning environment appropriate for gifted children. By 1956, the school had been converted into a school for the gifted. The IQ test was introduced and used, along with observations and interviews, to evaluate applicants for enrollment.

After becoming acquainted with a child, George and I began to estimate the applicant's IQ score. We understood that giftedness expresses itself in the emotional reactions of children, so we were not surprised when our independent assessment almost always coincided with the results of the IQ test, while offering important additional information. On many occasions, however, we found the test results to be much lower than our estimate. Usually, the tester herself felt that the IQ test result was not a true picture. It became more and more clear that the IQ test gave us only a partial answer— namely, one that revealed the cognitive abilities but not the emotional and spiritual characteristics of the gifted. I find this to be true to this day.

My husband and I retired from our work with the Roeper School in 1983 and moved to California, where we opened the Roeper Consultation Service for the Gifted, and we developed what was to become the Annemarie Roeper Method of Qualitative Assessment (QA). From that day forward, I have used this method to evaluate giftedness. I use it to help parents and schools to better understand gifted children and make appropriate decisions with them. Now in my 87th year and after seeing more than a thousand children, I feel it is important that others learn to use this method.

As time goes on, more and more experts have become interested in the QA approach, for they find it fills a gap. They need a way to evaluate children based on those characteristics that have not previously been considered—namely, the emotional and spiritual areas. A group of experts, which we named the Core Group, formulated the details of this approach. The Core Group was composed of specialists with relevant expertise—professors of gifted education, practitioners of QA, clinical psychologists, and directors of schools for gifted children—who have worked with me for many years and see the importance of this method.

Philosophy

If we are to understand children and their behavior, we must honor their inner world, relate to the unconscious as well as the conscious, and attend to the emotional as well as the cognitive. Education needs a clinical and developmental approach to assessment. My method of Qualitative Assessment uses a relational, experiential approach to facilitate the deeper understanding of individuals and thus nurture them in being more fully who they are. Through the QA method, we have found that because the emotional part of giftedness is not well understood, children can be erroneously labeled as pathological.

Many schools profess to serve the whole child and to provide appropriate educational approaches. However, they lack a legitimate, authentic method of assessing the whole child, of understanding the deepest wellspring of motivation and personality. QA fills this gap. It is a proven, rigorous means of experiencing the gifted child. It enables parents and teachers to more effectively open the door to learning opportunities and life experiences for the child. In this way, gifted children have greater potential to live their lives in a way that fully expresses who they are.

Approach

QA is used as an alternative to or in conjunction with traditional testing and offers a unique approach to the evaluation of giftedness. The wealth of information gained through QA is used to facilitate more effective planning for the education and parenting of children. It allows parents and teachers to better meet the needs of the children. It is based on an understanding of giftedness that looks beyond intellectual prowess or the ability to perform on an IQ test. The human psyche is enormously complex and not fully measurable by standardized psychometric examinations. The only instrument complex enough to understand a human being is another human being. QA practitioners use themselves as the instrument through which to understand the child or adult. QA offers a broader perspective to the assessment process, revealing the inner world of the individual. This method acknowledges the uniqueness of the individual, independent of the expectations of the practitioner, the school, or society.

By observing and reacting to a great variety of clues, including consideration of conscious and unconscious motivations, the practitioner replaces the conventional instrument of testing with his or her own finely tuned intuitive abilities to form an overall impression of the child. Central to the process is an attempt to understand the child's complex inner landscape. This understanding is supplemented by information and insights from the parents and the school, as well as the practitioner's own educational and psychological experience, empathy, and intuition. The practitioner also draws on her own knowledge and experience of the characteristics of gifted children, such as heightened empathy, a strong sense of justice with a need to right wrongs, perfectionism, acute sensitivity, intensity, and all-encompassing passion.

An essential element of QA is to provide an open and non-judgmental atmosphere in which the child has freedom of expression. The practitioner suspends judgment by letting go of all preconceived notions and giving, as Freud says, impartial attention to everything there is to observe. The intention is to create a relationship of trust between the practitioner and the child. The practitioner conveys to the child that the purpose of the meeting lies only in discovering—with the child's permission—who that child is, without expectations for any particular performance.

QA can be used to qualify children for placement in gifted programs and schools for advanced learners. It is extremely useful in designing programs, provisions, individual plans of development, and home education that nourishes the inner agenda, interests, emotional and spiritual development, and unique needs of the child. From insights gained about the child, the evaluator helps build a bridge to the appropriate educational resources available to the family. Evaluators help the family to construct their own educational path. The goal is to empower the child and the parents to take charge of their own destiny.

The Process of Evaluation

The QA process begins with the initial contact between the parents and the evaluator. It continues with the parent interview and ends with another interview with the parents. In between, there is the centerpiece: the interview with the child. This interview consists of emotional, spiritual, and cognitive experiences. Every part of this process is integral to the process itself.

For the evaluator, the process actually begins with the initial contact, whatever that may be: by telephone, via e-mail, in a letter, in person, or through referral from someone else. The evaluator has an immediate emotional and cognitive reaction to the person making the contact (usually the parent). Information is provided regarding age, family, schooling, concerns, etc. The trained observer begins to receive a flavor, a sense of the child, which later may be revised. The initial contact is a period of intense mutual evaluation, which later will be repeated with the child.

Mutual evaluation happens in any encounter between living things. It is often distorted by past experiences on the part of either party. The evaluator needs to be aware of these potential distortions in herself. There is, however, in most evaluators a vast reservoir of past experience that trusts in that intrinsic, uncontaminated knowledge within each person. This is a miracle in itself. Evaluators need to look at the whole process like a piece of art that is created by the encounter of the family, especially the child, with the evaluator. By the end, something new has been created—a dance, a work of art, a symphony. In the process, the soul of a child gets recognized, and the degree of giftedness of the child gets understood.

Initial Interview with the Parents

During this process, parents and evaluator create a common ground for mutual understanding and trust, allowing an image of the child's personality to grow among them. Within this framework, the evaluator attempts to gain as much information as possible about the child through interviewing the parents and reviewing background information offered in the parent questionnaire. Hopefully, channels of communication will open between the parents and the evaluator, thus creating a forum for cooperation to further address the needs of the family and child. Practical and emotional goals are discussed, such as school facilities and short- and long-range planning, and the evaluator discovers the expectations and the questions that the parents hope to have addressed.

The Child Encounter

For their inner safety, children need to have at least a cursory view of the environment. Children have a remarkable facility for making immediate judgments of individuals and situations. Their first impression may occur outdoors. They survey everything in a glance, with touching, with questions, or with silence.

The evaluator observes the way the child's counter-evaluation takes place. The manner in which the child appraises the situation is the first sign of the essence of the child. The child may be afraid, curious, anxious, calculating, comfortable, knowledgeable, etc. The evaluator receives this information about the child intuitively and through careful observation. The child's eyes are a most important clue. They may be darting all over the place while the child is doing something else. The time when the child is engaged in spontaneous evaluation of the situation is rich in emotional and cognitive information for the trained observer.

These are some of the questions that children need answered in their hearts:

✤ What is expected here?
✤ What is permitted?
✤ Must I be careful to protect myself?
✤ Are this person's intentions honorable as far as my soul is concerned?
✤ Can I trust this person with my inner agenda?

A desire to share or a need to protect may be born instantly. The child makes both unconscious as well as conscious choices. These are reactions that will have an impact on any type of evaluation—IQ tests, as well as others. With QA, there can be fewer emotional obstacles in the way of open expression and communication of thoughts and feelings. However, even those hindrances that remain offer clues to the essence of the child, as well as his or her giftedness.

In this initial stage, the child may answer questions selectively, picking out those that seem safe. Then there is an almost palpable moment when the child's counter-evaluation is complete. It feels as though the light or the air changes. Even though this process may never be completely over, if the evaluator passes the child's inspection, there is a clear sense of relaxation. From this moment on, the structure and content of the session flow effortlessly. Young children may use the toys available or those they brought from home. It becomes totally the child's agenda, even if it becomes repetitive and seems as if nothing is happening.

The goal is not for children to show how much they know or how bright they are, but to show who they are. This information presents itself in a pure form, almost like a byproduct. This is sacred information and must never be misused. Care needs to be taken by the evaluator not to interrupt the flow of expression by becoming impatient and thus influencing the course of events. Yet questions do have a place to encourage the child to convey what he or she really wants us to know. The interaction between the child and the evaluator is most valuable for the insights that the observer receives. The child may keep at a distance, seem to be oblivious of the evaluator, or get close, touch, talk trustingly, excitedly, and be eager to share. The secret is to further the flow of expression when needed, but not to change it.

Children draw, play games, and often talk for a whole hour, interrupted by occasional questions. As one of the characteristics of giftedness is overexcitability, the flow of information is often formidable. There are also situations in which the child is lost, as if in a trance, and never acknowledges the presence of the observer. Some are very slow in their actions, while others are extremely fast. Either can be a sign of giftedness.

The parents wait in another room. Occasionally, the child needs to check on them for his or her emotional safety. Sometimes one can feel that the child's attention is really with the family, especially if there is also a sibling waiting. Sometimes the child needs to go outdoors or to move. The events of the session are unpredictable and always a surprise.

The evaluator is not constrained by the clock-hour. It is desirable to keep the session to around an hour, but an hour and a half is not unusual. The observer gently ends the session by allowing a transition phase and observing that procedure. It is amazing for me to see how reluctant the children usually are to leave, even though I am old, cannot hear well, cannot get down on the floor with them, and do not have the latest toys. It is because they feel understood, recognized, and accepted. This experience, in itself, often becomes an important event for them, because they have been seen and recognized.

Keeping track as the session unfolds can be difficult for the evaluator. Having someone else take notes or recording the session helps the observer be present and open to taking in everything. As soon after the session as possible, so as not to lose any of the detail, the evaluator should write down impressions and record the emotional impact of the session.

Final Discussion

The final session with parents is equally important and handled in the same intuitive manner. Parents are deeply involved emotionally in everything concerning their children and need to feel recognized and understood for who they are as well. The same mutual evaluation process takes place. Mutual emotional acceptance and communication needs to occur. This session also includes specific recommendations for schools, family interactions, etc. These topics, too, are handled in the context of this new relationship with the evaluator, and a carefully written report may also be prepared.

Throughout the whole process, the evaluator gains necessary insights into the child's giftedness, personality, and inner world. She checks her observations against her experience, as well as her cognitive knowledge and awareness of the characteristics of giftedness. She knows that certain emotional and spiritual characteristics come with giftedness, such as overexcitability, perfectionism, sensitivity, sense of justice, etc. She knows that when a child worries about the concept of death at the age of three, he may be gifted. She takes all of this information into account in her evaluation.

The evaluator's knowledge of giftedness provides the cognitive information, and her intuition allows her a degree of certainty that she has received an accurate impression of the child. She has connected emotionally with the child and the parents, has trusted her intuitive insights, and is able to share her understanding of the child. Inherent in these results is always the recognition that one can never totally explore and understand another human being.

Further Thoughts on the QA Process

In trying to write this chapter, I am more and more assailed by contradictory thoughts and feelings about assessment itself, about our right and also our real ability to assess another human being. How are we qualified to judge each other, and what is the purpose of this judgment? Each Self is a mystery we can only penetrate down to just a little sliver of knowledge. We truly know so little about the human soul, about its enormous complexity and its relationship to the universe and to other souls. We know even less how to judge it. Why do we want to make these judgments? How do we want to use this knowledge? We need to be really clear about the reasons for this invasion of privacy. Do we want to use the child for our own purposes, using his talents for ourselves? Or do we want to help him find a place for his sacred Self in this world?

In the 40-plus years I have worked with gifted children, I have seen more than a thousand of them. I continue to be in awe of each young soul whom I am privileged to get to know. I have learned a great deal about each Self. I've experienced their emotions, anxieties, joys, passions, and ambitions, and I see that each Self is perfect in itself. It is only when we start comparing them to each other that we begin to see imperfection.

When we create norms against which to judge success and failure, achievement or backsliding, they are the result of some vaguely agreed upon sense of common reality. So we must understand that our evaluation results are basically arbitrary. We don't really have a common reality. Whatever we experience is from within the "I" of the beholder. No two people have exactly the same experience, nor can they actually share their experiences with each other. But human beings need guidelines, need to have a ground on which they can put their emotional feet. And so we have decided to create an arbitrary basis on which to measure people. How do we justify this measurement, and most of all, how do we know that we are correct, or even what would constitute correctness?

These are the questions we need to ask ourselves. And it's because I've seen so many children, each presenting an extremely complex unit, complete in itself and basically inaccessible to cognitive evaluation, that I am beginning to even doubt my right to make any kind of assessment.

In my work in the QA method, I have learned to see the soul of the child in itself, without the emotional layers imposed by our expectations and judgments. We do, however, create a common reality, and we judge others according to some often unspoken rules. One of the ways in which we evaluate children is by testing them in various ways. Many of these tests are designed to recognize a child's cognitive abilities and giftedness. In my work with gifted children, I have found that giftedness is based on emotions as well as cognition, hence my development and use of the QA method.

I have seen many highly gifted children who have had difficulties fulfilling society's expectations and who were therefore diagnosed with problems and disabilities. It is this realization that led me to develop the QA approach. I now believe that the word "assessment" may not quite represent the approach that I am using. I think we need to replace it with the concept of recognizing the individual Self, devoid of any attachments and expectations.

The next step after recognizing the Self of the child is recognizing the manner of integrating it into the world that surrounds us. It is for this reason that it became important to create a different approach to understanding each child so that we can help them to find their proper place. The purpose of QA differs from the purpose of other evaluation processes in that we are not looking for a judgment of ability, but a realistic understanding with which to keep this precious Self out of harm's way.

Few of the children that I see actually have IQ tests anymore, because most of the parents see Qualitative Assessment as a valid way of understanding their children. But whenever there is a comparison to the IQ test, it comes out to almost exactly the number that I arrived at. Actually, the reason parents like the QA approach is because it offers a real change in the expectations of parents who are interested in knowing *who* their child is and then finding the right environment for them, rather than knowing *what* the child can do.

As mentioned before, many of these children have difficulty fitting in to the expectations of the world around them. The more highly gifted they are, the harder it is for them to integrate. We have learned that through the QA method, we can recognize the degree of giftedness and the qualities that accompany the gifts. Knowing this helps us to find the best environment in which each soul may thrive.

So why did I spend my life assessing all these children? Because by doing this Qualitative Assessment, I find the characteristics that are the basis for the way these children live their lives, and by knowing them, we can help them to find their own place in the world. This, in turn, can allow children to grow and become an asset to society, changing it rather than being seen as a problem and an outsider.[18]

Chapter 11

My Own Personal Journey

In this chapter, I will address why I had to write this book, some of my memories of the development of my emotions, my awareness of unexpected unconscious reactions to the world around me, and what I have learned about myself through my work with children. I use myself as an example of the encounter with the outer world.

Recently, tears have been coming to my eyes, triggered by words or thought. Their origin is unknown to me. There is no specific feeling attached to them, just a kind of beautiful sadness. Maybe I am preoccupied at the moment with the concept of the unconscious because I am so aware of not knowing my own depth, the wellspring of my emotions. In fact, many of my emotions have been covered up. I lacked permission to express them, or rather I feared that they would be unwelcome in their intensity.

Recently, I bought a little statue made by a native of Africa. It comes from a village populated by artists carving images out of hard stone. It portrays the protection of the soul. Human beings find many ways to protect their soul. I am aware of having done this all my life. Something told me my soul did not matter much, but it was strong; it had a shine of its own, and it was not to be deterred. As I grew older, it seemed to stir and stretch and let me know of its growing presence. It now has to be reckoned with consciously. In the past, it made its presence felt daily through an urgency of inner needs which I was helpless against. It found its expression in an ever-present undercurrent of anxiety and sadness which seemed to live side by side with my active life. I would like to try to understand my soul as it interacted with the experiences of my life.

I remember little from my earliest years, but thinking of them evokes a sweet, loving feeling. I must have felt very safe and protected by my mother, held at her breast that fed me for the first two years of my life and kept the realities of food-poor Vienna from affecting me. In the past, when I tried to look back at my early life and listened to the stories that surrounded my childhood, I seemed to have a different focus. I was not sure that I played a large role in my mother's busy life. Now, however, I have a sense of being sweetly and deeply protected and that I loved my mother's physical closeness. I could always experience her through smell and taste. I think I loved her with a glorious passion and felt sweetly and totally protected, and maybe that is where my soul got its basic strength and health, allowing my creativity to slowly evolve over the years.

I do not want to let go of this feeling, this love for my mother. I cannot substantiate it with any factual memories. I have another feeling about it: I think I recognize my soul as something pliable and gentle and basically strong and sound. I also recognized my soul as paper-thin and exposed to the harshness and tenderness of the world. I was always on the edge of not believing I had a right to exist. Was I even existing? I always felt a tentativeness about myself.

My early childhood is devoid of facts and has a luminous twilight tone about it. Then I find myself emerging, maybe at age three—a fog begins to lift, and the sense of wonder, coupled with the existence of fear, becomes stronger. This sense of wonder is a feeling that never left me and increases in strength as I grow older.

Over the years, I imagined my bond with the world to be a rope with strands intertwined containing my deep anxieties, wishes, and forbidden dreams. It did not contain happiness, but so much passion and a joy within darkness and light. But mostly it contained sadness, which represented my hold on reality, as did my attachment to illness as a reservoir for overflowing stress.

At an early age, I became an accomplished daydreamer. This helped me solve some of the puzzles of this mysterious world and created a more comfortable and safe reality than my outside world, where I was never sure of being included or wanting to be included. Early on, I struggled with the concept of death—its mystery and attraction. It became the symbol for my awareness of the unknown and its place in the center of all humanness.

When I was very young, I heard someone say, "Everything is relative; nothing is absolute." These words increased my confrontation with the universal mystery. I was around six when I was overwhelmed with having to confront this concept. At about that age, a young boy, who had been my companion in the sandbox, died. I did not cry. I was just so astounded. I remember it adding another piece to the mystery. But I was troubled and more astounded at the reaction of other children. They acted happy, they played boisterously. Even then, I sensed that they were accomplished deniers. They had learned not to face the truth. It was a lesson I never learned in my intellectual mind, though I did learn how to keep it from hurting me by denying it access to my feelings. Unlike the other children, I thought deeply about death but did not feel it. Many times in my life, this helped me bear the knowledge of the truth. All this served to make me feel like an outsider with a deep desire to be inside.

My evening terrors must have started at that time, for how could I know that I would survive the night? But it was more than that—it was a fear of life as well as death. A wonderful byproduct was that often, when I went to bed, my elusive, handsome, royal-looking father would sit on my bed in order to console me. I don't remember many times alone with him when his attention was totally, benignly on me. I loved and admired him deeply; we were both philosophically inclined. I had a fantasy that there was a deep bond between us—that we shared a secret sadness.

Did he love me really? I do not think he noticed me much when I was a child. I have some kind of feeling that he spanked me on occasion. I cannot believe this, though, because it would be entirely against my parents' free-thinking philosophy. But the thought has always been in my mind. Did it happen? I do not know.

More likely, my nurse, who did not like me, told me it would happen if I did not behave.

I was usually a docile child, yet I was given to outbursts of temper tantrums. Temper tantrums are the only means of expression available to the child who develops an early superego based on clearly understood experiences, or to the child who fears losing tenuous love, or to the child who identifies so strongly and with so much empathy that she cannot hurt another person in words or deed. All of these might be said about me to some extent. I do not remember being angry at people or wanting to hurt anybody—I just remember the great frustration at not having some of my needs fulfilled. I think that I always felt that if I did not get attention, it was my fault.

Connecting my inner life with the outside world has always been a conscious issue for me. This was facilitated, however, by the fact that I had the opportunity to grow up in a community that was created by my parents—a community centered around the nurturing and understanding of personal relationships. This made it possible for me to integrate my inner world with the life around me, especially because all this happened within a very unusual physical environment consisting of miles of purple heather intermixed with birch trees. My canoe lived on a little pond adjacent to the so-called millhouse, where, off and on, our electricity was produced (half the time it was out!). It had a dream-like quality that allowed me to pursue my secret fantasy life and made my ever-present feeling of disconnectedness somehow bearable. I look back on it as a good, exciting, intellectually and emotionally fulfilling period of my life.

I really had what most people in the world don't have. And then, when it ended so suddenly and utterly, it really damaged my soul. When I had to leave Germany in 1939, I felt that my existence had been cut into two unrelated lives: my wonderful pre-Nazi childhood in Germany in the school community founded by my parents, followed by the terrible experience shared by millions of having to leave my home, my deep roots. In one blow, our world was totally destroyed by the Holocaust. I can remember today the very moment when a part of me died. I knew that my heart would break if I actually felt the pain, and I felt how my ability to feel turned itself off. The trauma was such that my emotional life seemed to have ended.

I felt reborn at age 21 in my new home in the United States. With great passion, my husband George and I set out to recreate a school similar to that founded by my parents—a community here in this country. Roeper School was the result. We had our own family and worked with thousands of children. It was a good and productive life.

George and I made many visits to our old school in Germany, and though the two parts of my life seemed to move closer and closer and a friendship sprang up between me and the school's leadership, there still continued to be an empty inner space of painful disconnectedness. I never expected the gap to close. This year, however, my miracle happened. For close to 40 years, I had come to Germany still feeling separated from my past. The German school invited me to visit and again received me with open arms. More than ever, there were conversations about what had happened to us when we left, and I felt their empathy. Although it has changed somewhat, the place still looks much as it did in my childhood: the little pond, the Neetze River, the mill— these are unchanged. And one day, as I was looking out at the little pond which had survived all these years, all of a sudden, a miracle seemed to happen. Just as years ago my life seemed to have split apart, it felt as though the two trains of my life had hooked up again and became one—I was home again! Words will never express how it feels to again have one life, uninterrupted and connected. Emotions now flow freely in me, unhindered. Sadness and happiness now have direct access to my heart, and I have since experienced both many times, and deeply.

The fact that my work, which is expressed in the Qualitative Assessment method, centers totally around the Self comes from the fact that I've spent many years looking for my own self!

Chapter 12

Growing Old Gifted

Much has been said, written, and researched about gifted children and adolescents. Yet there is a dearth of information when it comes to the gifted adult, and giftedness in old age has yet to be mentioned at all. There are many stories about old people: about their loneliness, their surprising longevity, and their ability to continue to participate in social life. In other words, much is said about how they stay young, but not much how they actually grow old. I've seen many people get old and die. Yet I don't even really know what old age is anymore.

What comes after adulthood? Seniorhood? Isn't that just an older adult? What defines a senior? Getting old and dying keep being postponed. I used to think that old age began at about the age of 70. Then people began to stay younger older (or did my perspective just change as I myself aged?). Well, I am too old to figure that out, but I know there is an astonishing difference between my grandparents at 70 and my generation. It is as though the end of the road has moved farther and farther out as I have traveled it. Being an adult covers an ever-larger span of time. People in their seventies are still fully functioning adults, deeply rooted in the day-to-day reality of our world.

Even into our seventies, there is little time to ponder life, death, and eternity—mankind's eternal concerns. We postpone these thoughts until later. But upon arrival in our early eighties, the road that we have been traveling—once well-lit, well-described, and well-worn—

begins to peter out until we are left standing in a field, no longer sure of the way. Older old age has not been described well except as a lack of young age. Now that I am 87, I feel that I'm on virgin ground, and there is not much, as far as I know, that can help me and others cope with our experiences.

Most of what I read and observe is based on the idea of staying young as long as we can. While the adolescent is looking forward to being an adult, the old person is trying hard to remain at the stage of the fully capable and participating adult. Much of what I call older old age consists of cumulative losses. You may lose your spouse, your friends, and your relatives (many of whom you've known all your life). You lose many of your capacities: your eyesight, your ability to hear; your sense of smell, your driver's license, and at least some of your memory. You also lose status and respect.

Old age is a time of loss; it can't be denied—it should not be denied. But many people try in diverse ways to hold on with all their might to their past status. Old age is also a time when people begin to get confused. I feel that the confusion might be part of the denial: "If I can no longer really understand the loss, it may not hurt so much." I personally want to experience this period with open eyes. When you're old in our society, you don't really count anymore. You feel demoted. This is a huge problem, actually typical for our society. The rug is pulled from under our feet. I am elaborating on this because I am literally in the middle of this.

So how does one find oneself? Or rather, how do we find our new position in life? Is it a new period of dependency? In some way, it is a repetition of childhood, only instead of having a growing body which is geared toward attaining independence, we have a disintegrating body. We can never know how far we are going to sink. When we are children, we look forward to building up, to gaining. At old age, however, we don't know how far the deterioration is going to go, and if we are gifted, we are especially inclined to watch it with open eyes.

When we are younger, we learn to compensate for our deficiency. We try to fix whatever may be wrong. As we get older, we can't continue to compensate for everything that we might lose. Rather, we find a way to face the ongoing losses, and we learn how to cope with what we can't compensate for. Some people find ways of accepting the losses by putting them into a religious framework ("It's God's will"). One of the ways the gifted have to cope with life is to look at whatever happens in a most honest way. The gifted do not necessarily seek ways in which to cover up these losses or to compensate for them.

Maybe that's the task of the gifted older old person: to look at things as they are, without trying to compensate or replace. I will never be young again. I will never drive a car again. My life on this planet is definitely moving toward its very end. This is probably the last stage of my life. Some of my dreams will not ever be fulfilled. In fact, one of the things we give up at old age, or perhaps sooner, is that we have witnessed plenty of change but not much progress, except in certain areas. It's not true that everything fits into neat dichotomies— good and bad, right and wrong. The universe defies explanation; life itself cannot be explained.

When we reach old age, we have to start giving up some of our hopes. In old age, we realize that we can't change the universe. Though we may make a great impact on a small part of it, even that impact comes to be seen in the context of a vast, unknowable universe. We don't have the capacity to really understand life and the universe, but there are ways in which we express that lack of understand-ing—through poetry, music, and art. These forms of expression resist interpretation. They are mysteries of our own creation.

When we are young, we hope that we will find the stone of wisdom. We spend all our lives trying to crack open the secret of life. In the process, we learn and invent an amazing amount of knowl-edge. Our vast knowledge has changed the face of the earth. Yet we have never discovered the secret of the universe. We scrambled along blindly, creating havoc but also much beauty. We are search-ing, forever driven by a need to know and create, like busy little ants.

From my window, I see two highways. Day and night, thou-sands of cars travel back and forth, and above them is the beauty and mystery of the unknown—the stars, the sun and moon. I have lived on this planet for 87 years but have not come any closer to answering the question I have been asking every day of my life: "What is this life, this universe all about?" Now I know deep in my heart that I will never know the answer. I'm trying to explore this unusual perspective. I think this older old age outlives our framework of definitions. I've always had this feeling that I don't belong and that we can't really interpret the mystery because we don't have the capacity for thinking beyond the three familiar dimensions. With old age, we no longer have the ability to look forward to an imagined future. We can't fix it. And of course, this is a definition of death, the ultimate finality of fate.

There's no definition of where I am in life now. It's beyond old—and I can't write about it because I can't define it. I'm saying goodbye to the last stage that's definable. I have never felt this way before. I also feel that there isn't anybody who can identify with this. The other old people I know are either senile or too firmly rooted in the concrete! I'm living in a twilight world. There is a lack of definition. In younger years, you can get through these times by considering your future, but in old age, there is no more future to imagine. How can you live without the future?

Maybe being beyond old forces us to really understand that the mystery is a reality. What stretches beyond the door of death is an eternity of unknown. Eternity and infinity are concepts that young children often struggle with, but even they soon give up because they can't find the answer. During our active lifetime, we forget about it. We get so involved with day-to-day living that we don't see the mysterious universe around us. Living beyond old, with our eyes open, may force us to truly accept the reality of the infinite and eternal, as well as to continue to understand the fact that we can never really know the answer while we are on this Earth. So peeking around the door of death, I see the road to eternity and infinity as the reality I need to live now. From traveling miles and miles of earthly road, I have gained the wisdom to accept the unknown, not only as the past and the present, but also as my only future.

So my conclusion is that when you reach the age beyond old, your only reality is the unknown. This has actually always been true, but many have been able to avoid it up until this point. We don't even really know the past or the present, let alone whether what one feels as a living Self will remain as such or transform into further unknowns. Integrating these understandings as a reality may be the definition of "beyond old age."

Gifted elders have to keep their minds trained carefully and keep on using them. In fact, I think that the preservation of the mind has an additional task: it serves to maintain the Self and its independence. Keeping a sharp mind becomes a way of preserving one's freedom and control. Just as I consciously watch every step I take so that I won't fall, I watch every thought I think so that I can keep control. But the need for control is also a form of mistrust. There is a point at which we must give up that control, and the only people to whom we can trustingly give it up are those who love us unconditionally.[19]

As I reread this chapter, with which I have been struggling for a long time, I realize that I have accepted the modern concept of old age—namely, that there is really no place in our bustling reality for it. As we age, we become "seniors," not the "wise elders" whose advice is sought and respectfully listened to. We are put into retirement homes. In fact, our children put us there. We are often not considered fully responsible anymore.[20]

However, I am sure there are many among the elderly who have accumulated much wisdom, but no one asks their advice. Congress does not have a section for "elders." Occasionally, one hears of elder statesmen, but we have no official place for them. We don't hear in Congress, "The 'elder' stateswoman from Hawaii wishes to speak." What would happen if every administration had an elected council of elder statespeople? Of course, they may have the same limitations as others, but chances are that they might bring a spiritual dimension, a view from the greater distance. Most of all, elders have less of a personal agenda, because they have lived their life and done their work. They are retired.

What opportunities do we miss by not hearing our elders, and what heightened experiences do they miss by us not allowing them to play their appropriate role in society? How much wisdom goes down the drain unused? In personal terms, I probably have more opportunity to be heard because I am still active in my work with gifted children, and I am listened to because my knowledge is defined and specific. Let us just remember how many parents and grandparents take care of their grandchildren or great-grand-children. They are the unsung heroes. I would like to end my remarks with a salute to old age.

References

Csikszentmihalyi, M. (1994). *The evolving self*. New York: Harper Perennial.

Dabrowski, K. (1972). *Psychoneurosis is not an illness: Neuroses and psycho-neuroses from the prospective of positive disintegration*. London: Gryf.

Gibran, K. (1923). *The prophet*. New York: Knopf.

Wolf, A. D. (1989). *Peaceful children, peaceful world*. Altoona, PA: Parent Child Press.

Endnotes

1   A 56-minute DVD, *Across Time and Space*, describes how the German Jewish Bondy family founded the Marienau school in Germany to teach children to find success in solving problems through tolerant, nonviolent, workable school democracy. The tragic events of the Holocaust increased the family's dedication to their mission, that equal rights for all people—particularly children—should be a priority. This DVD is available from Searchlight Films, 2600 Tenth Street, Suite 102, Berkeley, CA 94710, phone (510) 845-4135 or info@searchlightfilms.org.

2   In this book, the terms "soul," "psyche," and "Self" are used interchangeably.

3   Action in the world is determined by the "I" of the beholder. This is where all individual action originates before it becomes shared action. Hitler's inner agenda ultimately resulted in the Holocaust, and Gandhi's resulted in the birth of passive resistance, which inspired Martin Luther King, Jr. and the Civil Rights Movement.

4   Csikszentmihalyi (1994, p. 24).

5   These connections may lead to results that were hoped for unconsciously, driven by the energy of the sender. For example, a woman, Katrina, wakes up and feels compelled to open her computer in the middle of the night. There is an e-mail from a friend, Julie, about a third friend, Martha, who is experiencing great inner stress over her husband who is ill in the hospital. Martha is all alone; Julie lives very far away and has no way to help. Out of nowhere, Katrina's name had come to Julie's mind. Katrina lives closer to Martha and has the opportunity to support her. The message really originated with Martha, who sent out an emotional SOS and unconsciously connected with Julie, who sent an e-mail to Katrina and at the same time sent such a strong emotional message that Katrina awakened and felt compelled to open her computer. Katrina calls Julie, and together they figure out a plan to help Martha. If they had relied on conscious contact only, nothing would have happened until the next morning or later, and Martha's moment of crisis would have gone unaided.

6   At this point, the question will arise: How do I know this is true? It is simply from experience that we find the way in which a particular child will begin to trust and stop crying. The answer is different for each child.

7 In fact, education in many schools still does not include considering feelings as part of their tasks.

8 Some of the areas of expanded reality that are discussed by some persons who work with gifted children are ESP, memories of previous lives, deja vu experiences, and prenatal memories. Many adults have a problem with such notions, however. When it comes to practical situations, we cannot think in ways other than that this reality is absolute and that deviation from it may be pathological or fantasy. Many gifted children, on the other hand, take their sensitivity and versions of reality for granted, and they can apply it in daily situations, just as they take for granted the computer and the TV. They actually experience the aliveness of trees and flowers (there are children who hug trees and are inconsolable if we cut them down). This may be the reason the gifted so often get into difficulties in school and in their daily life. The definition of reality is a true problem that for us as adults is very difficult to solve. However, it may be helpful for us to remember that reality is relative and not absolute, and that many so-called "coincidences" are not coincidences, but part of some (to us) unknown overall connectedness.

9 From my own experience, I believe that we can switch back and forth between an extended awareness that allows greater inner flexibility and a limited, encapsulated view or reality.

10 It is now beginning to be common knowledge that these childrens' senses extend beyond the normal.

11 Gibran (1923).

12 Dabrowski (1972).

13 One of the problems that arises out of this situation is that real learning disorders, which certainly exist, are often difficult to ascertain within this context.

14 Another area of conflict between teachers and children is the constant demand of book reports on what they've been reading. Many children, particularly the gifted, consider their literary explorations their private possession, and the demand to share it is felt as an invasion of privacy.

15 This view looks at human affairs as the key to a changed perspective. Every actual event is shadowed by an emotional reaction. Out of these emotional reactions, certain patterns of behavior develop.

16 Each person's emotional definition of reality motivates his or her behavior, because it is the lens through which he or she sees an actual situation. The imagined monster in the closet is part of the perceived reality, and this changes the view of the environment.

17 Wolf (1989, p. 33).

18 As a result of a grant from the Malone Family Foundation, the Roeper Institute makes available Annemarie Roeper Qualitative Assessment Demonstration DVDs to interested members of the gifted education community at cost. The DVDs document three complete, unedited sessions of Annemarie Roeper conducting her Qualitative Assessment method with three different gifted children. Each complete QA sub-set consists of an opening session with the parents, a session with the child being assessed, a closing session with the parents, as well as reflections by Annemarie Roeper on each of the sessions in a question-and-answer format by an observer with expertise in gifted education. Viewing or possession of these materials does not entitle an individual to claim that he or she is formally certified in the QA method. For more information on certification, please contact Roeper Consultation Services at (510) 235-3173. These materials are protected under copyright and all rights are reserved. Materials can be ordered from the Roeper Institute by contacting (248) 203-7321 or by clicking on the Roeper Institute tab at www.roeper.org. Please allow 4 to 6 weeks for delivery.

19 If we look at our whole life experience, and especially that of young children, we will find that often we impose our own agenda on them. The same is true for old people.

20 Of course, there are those elderly people who do not wish to burden their loving children and gladly turn decision-making responsibilities over to them.